WRITING
THE
FAMILY NARRATIVE

WRITING
THE
FAMILY NARRATIVE

By Lawrence P. Gouldrup

Library of Congress Catalog Card Number 87-70106
ISBN Number 0-916489-27-2

First Printing 1987
10 9 8 7 6 5

Printed in the United States of America.

CONTENTS

Dedicated to
those members of my family who went before,
are now here, and are yet to come.

Courage came to me from the height of the mountain, and with it came the dignity of manhood, and knowledge of the Tree of Life, for now I was a branch, running with the vital blood, waiting in the darkness of the Garden for some unknown Eve to tempt me with the apple of her beauty, that we might know our nakedness, and bring forth sons and daughters to magnify the Lord our God.

I saw behind me those who had gone, and before me, those who are to come. I looked back and saw my father, and his father, and all our fathers, and in front, to see my son, and his son, and the sons upon sons beyond.

And their eyes were my eyes.

As I felt, so they had felt, and were to feel, as then, so now, as tomorrow and for ever. Then I was not afraid, for I was in a long line that had no beginning, and no end, and the hand of his father grasped my father's hand, and his hand was in mine, and my unborn son took my right hand, and all, up and down the line that stretched from Time That Was, to Time That Is, and Is Not Yet, raised their hands to show the link, and we found that we were one, born of Woman, Son of Man, had in the Image, fashioned in the Womb by the Will of God, the Eternal Father.

(Richard Llewellyn, *How Green Was My Valley*)

PREFACE

This is a book for that person who is beginning to write a family history. I have not intended it as a textbook for the serious writer of fiction, nonfiction, or biography but as a guide for the genealogist or amateur family writer who, for his own personal pleasure, wants to leave an account of himself or a historical record describing his own family. While I have been careful to make the distinction between the historical family exposition--the analytical and interpretive family history--and the historical family narrative--the historical short story or novel (see Chapter 1: "What is Family Literature?" where the difference is illustrated), I have not made a clear distinction between writing a short family narrative or short story and writing a longer family narrative or historical novel. Even though I refer to many novels for examples of technique, I have presumed that the reader is either writing a historical family exposition or writing a short family narrative or historical short story.

Because I have assumed that my audience is the beginning family writer, I have illustrated the principles in this book with amateur writing that my students have produced over several semesters of a beginning creative writing course. That is not to say that I have ignored professional examples of expository and creative writing; in fact, every chapter in this book begins with excerpts from professional writing, which serve as a basic point of reference. Every beginner needs to recognize that professional writers have used the family as a subject for expositions, short stories, and novels, which should inspire us by giving us an idea of what is possible. But a beginning writer needs the comfort that only the work of a writing peer can offer. The student samples are not necessarily great literature, but they represent reasonable goals that almost any dedicated beginner can achieve. Finally, I have built this book around several families that lived and died over the last two centuries: the Wells, the Partridges, the Farrows, the Dauers, the Wallers, and the Trapps. They were not great people, but they did live; and in some ways this book is their story.

Serious writers of fiction, nonfiction, drama, or poetry have only infrequently used the family as their subject. Because we do not commonly consider family literature as a genre or type, teachers of creative writing courses spend little time discussing what constitutes a good fictional or nonfictional family piece. In fact, all too often we treat anything written about the family as the subject matter of the unpromising writer, the amateur who has no talent for nonfiction or serious fiction. This does little to inspire the average student in a creative writing course to write a family history. It is true that family literature (or specifically the nonfictional family exposition or narrative) is a good avenue for motivating the beginning writer who is short on ideas, but it is not the field for the careless writer. It requires commitment and careful preparation to write a readable family exposition or narrative, and few--teachers or students alike--understand the peculiar demands involved. The very factors that make it an appealing form of writing for the beginner present for the undisciplined writer hazards that all too often result in a tedious and unappealing product.

One hazard that many beginners fall victim to is the temptation to tell the complete story of the family, typically its origin in the Old Country, its humble beginnings in the United States, and its modern successes. Little appreciating the enormity of the task, undisciplined beginners produce a story marked by superficial breadth. Successful family writers, however, limit themselves to specific issues, persons, or periods. MacFarlane's expository history *The Family Life of Ralph Josselin* devotes itself exclusively to one aspect of Josselin's life. Sigrid Undsett in her novel *Kristin Lavrandsdatter* takes three novels to tell the story of a woman's life, hardly the complete story of a family. Vilhem Moberg's *The Settlers* covers only a limited period in a family's history and has a very definite focus. The beginning family writer must consider carefully the scope of his story, gather the necessary details to give the story sufficient depth, and limit himself to only what the known facts justify.

Usually, however, it is the genealogist who has compiled scores of pedigree charts and family group sheets and who, with literally hundreds of disjointed facts and details, blunders into writing a family history. With the increased enthusiasm for genealogical research and the ever-widening availability of local and family-history collections, many genealogists in a relatively short time gather information that fills up and goes far beyond the usual family group sheet or pedigree chart. It is all fascinating--at least to the genealogist who has compiled it; and now, as a family historian, he proceeds to bore his reader with every tedious detail. Ignoring all caution and flying in the face of good taste, he produces page after page of dreary and unrelated facts. But a good family exposition or narrative is not a long-hand form of the pedigree chart or the family group sheet. It is a carefully crafted and focused piece of writing built around a specific theme.

Perhaps the pitfall that claims most beginners is the almost universal human drive to protect those closest and dearest to them. Basically, it is the problem of what we should or should not tell about ourselves or our families. Many of us feel obligated to spare the readers the ignominy of our ancestors. I can offer no easy solution, but no one believes a "bowdlerized" or idealized version of someone's life. There are too many family histories that deal only with someone's goodness, courage, determination, or faith in God. On the other hand, many writers feel that no story is interesting unless it is filled with the shocking and the seamy. Perhaps the best approach is a compromise somewhere between the idealized and the sensational. After all, human beings are complex, a mixture of good and bad, and an emphasis on one or the other is a misreading of a life.

Deciding what is the truth and what is not the truth, however, is a much more complex problem and one that the writer of the family narrative must constantly face. It is really what Irving Stone addresses when at the end of *Lust for Life* he suggests that the reader may ask the question, "How much of this story is true?" Not being physically present at every conversation that Vincent van Gogh had, Mr. Stone could not conceivably have been able to know exactly what was said, and in "one or two instances" he portrayed incidents that he felt were probable but which he knew he could not document. When Truman Capote in 1966 set out to describe the murder of a Kansas family in his book *In Cold Blood*, he elected to tell his story as a "nonfiction novel." Norman Mailer in his 1968 account of a march on the Pentagon, *The Armies of the Night*, subtitled his work "History as a Novel, the Novel as History." All of these authors touched on a issue that poses a difficult problem for the family narrator. Basically Stone's, Capote's, and Mailer's approach is that an author, after careful research and thought, is in a position to reconstruct scenes and dialogue for which there is no documented evidence. In other words, many writers feel free, after acquainting themselves carefully with the subject or subjects of the narrative, to fabricate portions of the story that may not be technically correct but which do serve to advance the "truth" of the subjects of their stories. Perhaps Wallace Stegner, after piecing together the facts and details of a scene of which he had only circumstantial evidence, says it best:

> And now I can't avoid it any longer. I have to put words in their mouths. Not very personal words at first. Questions and answers. Probes. Time-fillers.

> (Wallace Stegner, *Angle of Repose*)

The suggestion that the family narrator at any point has the right to "put words in their mouths," to fabricate or fictionalize portions of the family narrative, or that he can capture the "truth" of a nonfictional account in carefully fictionalized scenes or dialogue will immediately raise the alarm of the traditional family historian or genealogist. After all, genealogy and family history have only recently emerged from the dark ages of pedigree fabrication, and few want to go back to the days when every pedigree had at least one king, two dukes, and Adam and Eve.

There are probably as many answers and opinions about this as there are writers, and, while there are many who feel that it is possible for the writer of the family narrative to cross that fine line between nonfiction and fiction without his feeling that he has violated the "truth" of a family narrative, the amateur writer of the family narrative will probably want to avoid straying too far from the historical facts. We will, however, come back often to this problem.

Basic to all good family history--exposition or narrative--is the principle of immersing oneself totally in the historical subject matter. Perhaps nothing is more important than this, and it is a sad but true fact that few writers ever really understand this principle. The successful family writer, whose expositions and narratives are widely read and enjoyed, leaves no lead unfollowed in attempting to understand his historical subject. There are many techniques that one must learn to control as he masters the writing of family history. This book covers those that relate specifically to the family exposition and narrative. Learning to write is an on-going process in which the author constantly learns, adapts, and relearns writing techniques. But there is no technique more important than the principle of giving oneself completely to the subject matter. Irving Stone makes this point graphically in the bibliography of *Those Who Love*. There are thirty general categories of sources that he has synthesized, and the total number of individual works he has consulted must run well into the thousands. It is almost impossible for anything but good exposition or accurate characterization and plot to result when the writer does that kind of research. Yet convincing writers that they need to expend the time and energy required is not easy. There is, though, a certain kind of hope that I have in the amateur family historian and genealogist because they of all people seem willing to devote themselves to the muses of family history. They have spent years leafing through forgotten manuscripts and slowly turning the handles of countless microfilm machines. They have stood in long lines at copiers waiting their turn to add yet one more page to their already voluminous files. They have felt what those who lived in the past have felt. They have understood. If you want to write good family history, you must be willing to give yourself first completely to family research.

The family history, then, is a form of literature--nonfictional exposition or narrative--that while attractive and appealing as subject matter contains natural hazards that can quickly condemn a writer's work to tedious banality. Hazards aside, all researchers should recognize that vital statistics, military records, probate documents, and census enumerations, in addition to yielding statistical data, can tell a very individual and human story. Too often, family researchers and genealogists have viewed their work as complete with the retelling of the pedigree-and-family-group-sheet facts and details in expository or narrative form. Nothing can be farther from good family literature. We should begin to see the need for the more complete human record: the crafted family history. I have written this book on the premise that the goal is not the unimaginative listing of the facts from the family group sheet or the pedigree chart but the sensitive rendering of a human being's story told with control and focus.

Finally, I am deeply grateful to personal family members--my wife Sandy and my mother-in-law Marjorie Thomas--as well as to my fellow teacher of creative writing and colleague Bill Johnson who read the manuscript and offered valuable suggestions and support. Without their help this book would not have been possible.

CHAPTER 1

WHAT IS FAMILY HISTORY?

After weeks, months, or even years of pouring over difficult-to-read microfilms and faded original documents, extracting names and dates, and reconstructing families on group sheets and pedigree charts, you are now ready to write a family history that will bring together in one final statement all that your family is and has experienced. If you are the typical family researcher, you are intimately acquainted with the various genealogical sources and techniques of research but have probably spent little or no time reading family histories, and as a result you have no clear idea of the range and scope of the family history much less what the elements of a good family exposition or narrative might be.

At the very outset, then, we need a working definition that will help us to distinguish between those works that are clearly family literature and those that touch on the family but do not qualify as family literature. For example, biographies and autobiographies are historical expositions or narratives that, in telling a person's life story, cannot avoid dealing with his family or with his relationship to his family; but touching on a subject's family does not automatically translate a biography or autobiography into family literature. It is really a matter of emphasis. Family literature, then, is that piece of writing--prose, poetry, or drama-- that *emphasizes* the family and that sees the individual as a part of the larger family unit whether over one or several generations. It does not casually touch on the family; it *focuses* on the family and sees its subjects as units within the family.

In drama, we find many plays that use the family as subject matter but do not focus on the family. August Strindberg's play *The Father* explores the power relationship of man to woman within the family setting; Tennessee Williams's *Cat on a Hot Tin Roof* deals with a family struggling with the passing of financial power from one generation to another, and Arthur Miller's *Death of a Salesman* shows the tragic decline of the modern work-a-day father of an American family. Yet of the three, only Miller's play comes close to family drama and thus family literature.

Miller is preoccupied with the father's—Willy Loman's—tragic decline, but at the end of the play there is the feeling that somehow the family will survive the death of the patriarch, a focus that is on the family not the father. William Shakespeare's *King Lear* and Beth Henley's *Crimes of the Heart* provide a fascinating comparison of familial conflict. Both of these dramas are built around the relationship of three daughters or granddaughters to a declining father or grandfather, in *King Lear*, from the father's point of view and in *Crimes of the Heart*, from the granddaughters' point of view. Both involve a familial crisis; Shakespeare's drama is centered around the father's need to maintain some kind of emotional and financial independence in his declining years in the face of two daughters who are determined to destroy his financial power, and Henley's play is centered around the granddaughters' need to establish their independence from an aged tyrant who has managed to convince one girl that she can never marry because of her shrunken ovary, another that she must marry a man that she eventually shoots in the stomach, and the third that she need deny herself nothing until her lack of self-discipline spells personal ruin. Both plays are possible only in the context of the family, and one could argue that these plays come close to family drama.

There are plays, however, that come even closer to qualifying as family drama. *Our Town*, by Thornton Wilder, emphasizes the family as well as the relationships of individuals within that family. Molly Newman and Barbara Damashek's *Quilters*, based in some respects on American local history, explores the role of women within the family setting. In *Buried Child*, Sam Shepherd, reaching back into his own childhood, explores startling and unpleasant themes. He delves into a secret that an emotionally disturbed family had shared and protected until that secret itself became the governing psyche of the family. Here we see plays that clearly focus on the family and are distinctly different from plays like Shakespeare's *Romeo and Juliet*, which, while dealing with a typical family crisis such as the elopment of an only and protected daughter, still emphasize the problem itself over the family.

Poetry has also been a medium for recording the events and emotions associated with the family. One year after John Rixman died in 1620, his wife Mary had a burial brass with a few lines of poetry erected to his memory. John, a fellow at Oxford, had given up his academic position to marry, and his wife remembered his sacrifice to the god of love in the following personal verse:

> When Oxford gave thee two degrees in art.
>   And love possest thee master of my heart
> Thy colledge fellowshipp thow lefs't for mine
>   And nought but deathe could seprate me from thine
> Thirty five yeares we livd'e in wedlocke bands
>   Conjoyned in our hearts as well as handes
> But death the bodies of best friends devides

> And in the earths close wombe their relyckes hides
> Yet here they are not lost but sown that they
> May rise more glorious at the judgment day.

Yet, while touching on the kind of love that developed into a strong familial bond, the poet has not written family poetry.

Wordsworth, in 1800, did follow a family theme in his pastoral poem "Michael"--in this case the rejection of parental values by a beloved son and the blow that rejection brought to the aged father and mother. Family property located in the Lake District of England is important in the poem. The owner, Michael, had with his wife cared for and developed the fields of his property into a choice inheritance that he hoped to pass on to his son as his father had passed it on to him. Through "misfortunes," though, the son had to go to London to earn enough money to recover the loss that was being levied against the property. Both father and son made a covenant of love symbolized in their together laying the first stone of the "Sheep-fold." The son started off bravely enough but soon gave himself "to evil courses" in the city and escaped his great sense of familial shame "beyond the seas," never returning to honor the covenant he had made with his father. The property was lost, and the family as a unit ceased to exist. Here the poet presents in poetic form the story of a family.

A contemporary example of the use of poetry to describe members of one's own family is Edgar Lee Master's *Spoon River Anthology*. Master's poetic portraits, of course, reach out far beyond his immediate family to an entire community, but his tribute to his grandmother, Lucinda, is an excellent example of family literature in poetic form:

> I went to the dances at Chandlerville,
> And played snap-out at Winchester.
> One time we changed partners,
> Driving home in the moonlight of middle June.
> And then I found Davis.
> We were married and lived together for seventy years,
> Enjoying, working, raising the twelve children,
> Eight of whom we lost
> Ere I had reached the age of sixty.
> I spun, I wove, I kept the house, I nursed the sick,
> I made the garden, and for holidays
> Rambled over the fields where sang the larks,
> And by the Spoon River gathering many a shell,
> And many a flower and medicinal weed --
> Shouting to the wooded hills, singing to the green valleys.
> At ninety-six I had lived enough, that is all,
> And passed to a sweet repose.
> What is this I hear of sorrow and weariness,
> Anger, discontent and dropping hopes?

> Degenerate sons and daughters,
> Life is too strong for you --
> It takes life to love life.
>
> (Edgar Lee Masters, *Spoon River Anthology*)

One portrait does not tell the entire story of the family, but a poet could with several poetic portraits produce a piece of writing that is family poetry and hence family literature. While both poetry and drama can qualify as family literature, neither has been a popular medium for presenting a family, and neither fits the common definition of family history. Later, we will consider several poems that are valid records of a family, but the fact is that it is normally through prose narration that writers have told the story of the family.

Basically, there are two kinds of prose options that qualify as family history: the exposition and the narrative. Exposition is the form of prose that we write in beginning English courses and is normally what is meant when we think of the term paper. The starting point for all exposition is the thesis or controlling idea. Some see the controlling idea as part of the thesis. However one defines it, the writer begins with something that he or she is attempting to prove or establish about a subject. Henry S. Bennett's *The Pastons and Their England* is an example of this technique:

> Yet as we have said, John Paston was primarily a calculating, shrewd man of affairs, and most probably only a servant of the County, because he recognized that in the main the interests of the County and his own were identical. His whole energies were absorbed in the double adventure. The zeal and capacity he showed were not wasted, for he early attracted the attention of just such a man as his growing fortunes most needed.
>
> (Henry S. Bennett, *The Pastons and Their England*)

The author states clearly that he is going to establish that John Paston was both "shrewd" and "calculating" in conducting his personal and business affairs. The task that then follows is to provide the necessary support and detail that will convince the reader that the author's basic thesis is valid. In providing support for a thesis, an author first finds ideas that confirm the general thesis (often designated as topic sentences). Second, he provides details for those support ideas.

Bennett does this over and over again in his book. In discussing the life of a woman, he sets his thesis out clearly at the beginning of Chapter 5: "The medieval marriage . . . was very much a matter of business . . ." One of the sentences supporting this general thesis is that the wife's "real function was the ordering and proper management of the house." He then breaks this support idea down into several specific functions: spinning, growing, preparing and preserving food, and bargaining. And in each case he provides specific details; one example is Paston's wife's letter to her husband asking him to purchase some necessary cloth:

> I pray you that you will . . . buy some frieze to make your child's gowns. You shall have best cheap and best choice of Huy's wife as it is told me. And that you will buy a yard of broad-cloth of black for an hood for me at 3/8 or 4/- a yard, for there is neither good cloth nor good frieze in this town.
>
> (Henry S. Bennett, *The Pastons and Their England*)

Another example of the historical family exposition is Alan MacFarlane's *The Family Life of Ralph Josselin: A Seventeenth-Century Clergyman*, which analyzes the life cycle, the social world, and the intellectual world of the seventeenth-century clergyman using the lives of Ralph Josselin and his family as examples. The section below, which considers the relations within the family, is typical of MacFarlane's approach:

> Some of the general features of the Josselins' relations with their children have already been described: their treatment of them as infants and children until they left home to become educated as servants or apprentices between the ages of ten and fifteen; the degree to which they controlled and financed their children's marriages; the way in which wealth was transmitted in a series of gifts at apprenticeship, marriage and the parents' death. We may therefore turn to more specific ties, those between father-daughter, mother-daughter, father-son, mother-son. The evidence is more complete for daughters, five of whom survived beyond childhood as against two sons. The fact that historians have tended to be more interested in father-son relationships, makes a case for exploring daughter relationships first.
>
> (Alan MacFarlane, *The Family Life of Ralph Josselin:* A Seventeenth-Century Clergyman)

The exposition can succeed or fail on several points: Is the thesis clearly stated? Do the sub-ideas or topic sentences relate to the basic idea being established in the thesis? Are there adequate details to establish the sub-ideas or topic sentences? There are also several rhetorical forms that exposition can take. We can provide examples, explain a process, classify, show a causal relationship, argue, or compare and/or contrast. Yet, basically, all of these forms are built on the clearly stated thesis. If the author has not taken the time to establish in his own mind what it is that he is attempting to show or prove, the exposition will be a hopeless mass of confusing and contradicting specifics.

Much of what we will consider in Chapter 2: "Using Genealogical and Local History Records to Write the Narrative" involves works that analyze rather than tell a story, and the thrust of Chapter 2 is to show the family writer how to analyze original sources so that he can write a good family history. Chapter 3 advances to writing the family narrative, and, while I am convinced that the author must first acquaint himself with good general or familial analytical histories and master the techniques of writing a decent analytical history before he can write a good narrative, the family narrative is a distinctively different form.

The family narrative is a story. It is not, as in the case of the historical family exposition, a political, cultural, social, or economic analysis; it is simply a story about a family or about a person in a family setting. What is confusing is that there are those books that take of both elements, historical exposition and narrative, making it difficult at times to know whether we are dealing with a family exposition or a family narrative. Actually, there is no reason why a person could not write a book that is both a family history and a family narrative providing he included both elements, analysis and story. Generally, though, it is one or the other; and it is relatively easy to see the difference. Vilhem Moberg's *The Emigrant Saga* is a narrative about a young couple that leaves Sweden in 1850 to settle in Minnesota. There are no discussions about the Swedish intellectual or social world; there is a series of events leading to some kind of resolution. The section dealing with Karl Oskar's butchering of the ox to save his son's life is an example of a family narrative:

> At last the carcass was clean. Karl Oskar had prepared a warm, safe room for his son.
> He pulled Johan out from under the cart, carried him to the ox and placed him inside the carcass. There was plenty of room in there for the child, and the warm body would revive the boy. Then he folded the edge of the hide over the child, who was coming to life from the heat.
> "Are we home, Father?"
> "Yes, Go to sleep again, boy."
>
> (Vilhem Moberg, *The Emigrant Saga*)

In recent years, we have seen numerous examples of the family narrative or story, the most notable being Alex Haley's *Roots*. *Roots*, however, is really only a recent manifestation of a long-standing literary tradition that reaches back into ancient times with a focus on the royal families. This tradition passed from the ancient to the modern worlds in works such as the dramas of Aeschylus and the epics of Homer and Virgil. Aeschylus's *Oresteia*, a dramatic trilogy, follows a royal family through three generations of murder and blood vengeance. Homer's *Odyssey* is the story of one man's struggle to return home to a wife and a son who are locked in a daily combat to preserve the integrity of their family against audacious suitors and insolent servants. The final scenes of the *Odyssey* involve the moving reunion of father and son and the tender recovery of love between Odysseus and his wife Penelope. Virgil's *Aeneid* begins with Aeneas carrying his father on his shoulders and leading his son by the hand emphasizing that this is really the story of the immortality of the family. While all of these ancient works were extremely important for developing in the Western world a continuing interest in the family, it was the King James Version of the Bible that formalized and stabilized for the English-speaking world the ancient family literature of the Hebrews, which more than any literature ensured a continuing Western interest in the family. This ancient literary preoccupation, gradually shifting from the noble to the common family, developed on this continent into what we know as American regional and local-color literature. In the nineteenth century, the infusion of the immigrant further developed this emphasis on the family, resulting in the pervasive and widely popular immigrant story.

Chronologically the first and single most important influence for the Western world began with the oral tradition that was later written and collected into the religious books and stories of the Old Testament. While most persist in seeing books such as Genesis as a theological statement or as badly-garbled history, few have ever seen it for what it actually is: a family narrative. It begins with the story of Adam and Eve, advancing rapidly to the story of Noah and his family. This historical preface is only a backdrop for the real heart of Genesis: the story of Abraham's family over several generations. Abraham and his wife Sarah finally have a son, Isaac, whom Abraham almost--on God's command-- sacrifices. Isaac survives to sire two sons, Jacob and Esau, who spend years misunderstanding each other, reconciling themselves ultimately in the presence of Jacob's now large and impressive family. And Jacob's family story--mainly a focus on his son Joseph--is a moving climax to the account of bitterness, reconciliation, and family survival. Even the framework of the story of Jesus as found in the Gospels of Matthew, Mark, and Luke is familial. It begins with a genealogy showing the broader familial context, proceeds chronologically through Jesus' youth to adulthood, and culminates in Jesus' ministry and death. Our Western scriptural heritage--the Bible--makes the point over and over again in recurring chapters of the same story that it is easier to conceptualize history and even moral and theological precepts in the framework of the family story.

The second important development that the ancient literary interest in the family took was in American regional and local family literature, a natural outgrowth of our European origins and the geographic regions of America. There were, generally speaking, two western movements in the United States--one centered in Indiana and one in California--with Edward Eggleston representing the first and Mark Twain and Bret Harte representing the second. Both Harte and Twain brought to life the excitement and vitality of the gold-rush era, which increased our understanding of common people in ordinary situations, but it was Twain in his *Adventures of Huckleberry Finn*, actually an example of southern regional literature, who achieved true greatness in telling the story of a young boy who spent a good deal of his youth fleeing from a drunken father eventually to encounter what he considers to be the far worse fate of being adopted and "sivilized" by Aunt Sally. Twain's masterpiece is many things to many people, but it is clearly impossible to think of Huckleberry Finn without thinking of Huckleberry's family. Another writer of southern regional literature, and certainly a writer of far less stature, was John Pendleton Kennedy who, in his *Swallow Barn*, depicted the tranquil country life of a southern family. Sarah Orne Jewett showed us vignettes of Maine family life in her *Country of the Pointed Firs* (which deals with women along the coast of Maine) and in her *A Country Doctor* (which she probably intended as her autobiography). These and various other regional novels did much to acquaint us with the family life of local regions that were long forgotten. Harriet Beecher Stowe's *The Pearl of Orr's Island* is, like Jewett's novels, a story about Maine and Maine family life. Her *Poganuc People* authentically depicts in scene after scene local and familial Connecticut history. And her *Oldtown Folks* depicts, through personal glimpses of common family life, her struggle with the religion of New England. Another writer in this vein was Rose Terry Cook whose *Root Bound*, as with most if not all of these novels (if we can use the term novel), strikes us as maudlin. Yet they all advanced the form of the family narrative.

The literature of the immigrant, the third major development and itself an influence in the adaptation of the family theme in the United States, traditionally begins in the post Civil War period, although examples of immigrant literature can be traced back almost to the beginning of the first settlements on the American continents. After all, the English, Spanish, and French colonists were themselves immigrants in a new and uncharted world, and many kept what is plainly a personal and family record: the Quaker John Woolman's journal, the Puritan Samuel Sewall's diary, and the southern aristocrat William Byrd's secret diary. Nevertheless, it was after the Civil War that writers began depicting the non-English immigrants that now flock from Europe. O.E. Roelvaag dealt with Norwegian immigrants in his *Giants in the Earth*, and Willa Cather touched on the Quebec French in her *Shadows on the Rock*, the Norwegians in *O Pioneers*, and the Nebraska Czechs in *My Ántonia*. Vilhelm Moberg, after World War II, followed in this tradition with his series of novels on Swedish immigrants in Minnesota: *The Emigrants, Unto a Good Land, The Settlers*, and *Last Letter Home*.

These three literary and historical developments--the narratives of the Bible, regional and local literature, and the immigrant story--inspired and focused the American interest in writing about the family, which reached its most recent stage of development in the increasingly popular family novel, the most obvious example of which is Alex Haley's novel *Roots* (published in 1976). In turn, *Roots* itself brought about a renewed and heightened interest in the family narrative. In actuality, the modern family novel had been around for several years although it had clearly not captured the public's interest in the way *Roots* did. Many authors before Haley had dealt with the family: Thomas Mann (1901) in his *Buddenbrooks*, Galsworthy (1922) in his trilogy *The Forsyte Saga*, and Wallace Stegner (1971) with his *Angle of Repose*. However, it was Alex Haley's portrayal of a black family's origin and existence that gave for most of us the clearest statement of what the family narrative is and can be. In telling the story of a plainly common, immigrant family over several generations, Haley relied on research both into genealogical records and family oral history, sources that most average Americans could and would turn to for information about their ancestors. These family stories encourage local and regional awareness that reminds us all of the small-town background from which the average American family has normally come. Its power, however, sprang from the almost epical and Biblical quality of the narrative as Haley told a story that evoked the strange and distant echoes of the ancient epic of Abraham's family in Genesis.

Family history, then, has been a prose account--exposition or narrative--in which the primary focus is the family as a unit. It sees the family whether common or grand--the norm today is clearly the common--over several generations. It derives its vitality from authentic regional awareness and understanding and its reality and sense of historical accuracy from sound historical and genealogical research. Particularly with the family narrative, it sees its subject as an epic of the modern common man, as a migrating everyman who has emerged out of the mysterious past to contribute its strand to common threads that make up our historical past and national present.

Before the writer dare take pen in hand, he must acquaint himself with successful family histories so that he might develop a personal standard of what a good exposition or narrative is, as well as decide which techniques and approaches have worked well for others and might work well for him. After all, no one can afford the luxury of ignoring what others have written, particularly if he expects to have readers understand and appreciate what he writes. Because our goal is the exposition or the narrative--not poetry and drama, the beginner must acquaint himself specifically with prose. The following bibliography considers primarily prose--specifically the family exposition, autobiography, biography, journals and diaries, and the family narrative. It is highly selective and illustrative only ,although I have focused on works that represent the historical periods and geographical areas about which most would be writing and which provide a significant sampling of subject matter, author, and technique. I recommend that the beginning writer read most if not all of these works so that he can become closely familiar with all kinds and types of family history. As he reads, he will discover other prose examples that may relate more directly to what he is writing, but the works that follow are a good place to start. The wise writer builds on the examples and techniques of those who have gone before, and once he understands what others have done, he can choose and adapt techniques that work for him.

AN ANNOTATED BIBLIOGRAPHY: WRITING ABOUT THE FAMILY

EXPOSITION: ANALYZING THE FAMILY

Bennett, Henry S. *The Pastons and Their England*. Cambridge: The University Press, 1951.

Basing his analysis on the Paston Letters, Henry S. Bennett examines the Paston family from many points of analysis: marriage, love, women's lives, parents and children, houses and furniture, education and books, letters and letter-writing, roads and bridges, wayfaring, the law, lawlessness, religion, the secular clergy, the regular clergy, and the life of the countryside. It is actually a consideration of life in fifteenth-century England.

MacFarlane, Alan. *The Family Life of Ralph Josselin: A Seventeenth-Century Clergyman*. New York: W.W. Norton and Company, 1970.

MacFarlane prefaces his treatment of Ralph Josselin with a discussion of the purposes and functions of the diary in seventeenth-century England. Only a minor portion of the book is devoted to a biography of Josselin, the majority being an analysis of the life cycle, the social world, and the intellectual world of the seventeenth-century clergyman. It is an excellent example of family exposition.

AUTOBIOGRAPHY: WHAT MY LIFE HAS MEANT TO ME

Baker, Russell. *Growing Up*. New York: Congdon and Weed, 1982.

A charming autobiography with elements of biography. Baker limits his autobiography as the title suggests to his early life up through his marriage. Because he focuses on his early life, he includes a warm portrait of his mother.

Cellini, Benvenuto. *The Autobiography of Benvenuto Cellini*. Garden City, N.Y.: Doubleday and Company, 1946.

Cellini wrote his autobiography between 1558 and 1566, beginning when he was fifty-eight. He felt no one should begin an autobiography until he was at least forty. His book, which sheds light on all aspects of sixteenth-century life in Florence, Italy, is filled with all the inconsistencies and contradictions of a man caught in conversation, although he includes some delicate and powerful character descriptions.

Frank, Anne. *The Diary of a Young Girl.* Garden City, N.Y.: Doubleday and Company, 1952.
Anne's diary covers her life from thirteen to fifteen, a period of important personal changes for a young girl. What makes her personal story all the more poignant, of course, is the fact that her family hid during the Nazi occupation of Holland literally unknown by and not knowing the outside world. It is a powerful diary of a young girl who sustains herself with her personal charm and wit during a most terrifying time.

Jewett, Sarah Orne. *A Country Doctor.* New York: Meridian Classic, 1986.
This novel--considered to be the author's autobiography--explores the very modern theme of a woman having to choose between marriage and a career as a Maine country physician. The book, primarily important as an example of the regional novel, contains charming portraits of old Maine houses and furnishings, country scenes with congregations of flowers, local gossip and outings, and the changes in the sea and the weather. Jewett's book reminds us of the principle that for a family narrative to be convincing, it must contain true on-the-spot descriptions.

McCarthy, Mary. *Memories of a Catholic Girlhood.* New York: Harcourt Brace and World, 1952.
As the title suggests, this is the autobiography of an orphaned girl who undergoes all the incidental trauma of losing her family and finds a safe but disturbing spiritual home in the Catholic faith. Her autobiography, an arresting analysis of the "mystery and wonder" that faith provided her, leads inevitably to what she defines as a life of "lapsed" Catholicism.

Roosevelt, Eleanor. *The Autobiography of Eleanor Roosevelt.* New York: Harper and Brothers, 1961.
Eleanor Roosevelt gives a picture of the world in which she grew up as well as a picture of herself. She covers the influences of the values of the world of her youth, her husband's political life, and her participation in the building of international understanding. In the concluding part of the book, her observations provide meaning and understanding to her immensely vital life.

Steinbeck, John. *Travels With Charlie.* New York: Viking Press, 1962.
John Steinbeck uses his travels with his dog Charlie through the major regions of the United States to explore his own personal psyche as well as the national psyche of America. The book is hardly the standard autobiography with its focus on a journey, but it contains enough

references to Steinbeck's attempt to find the truth about America to qualify as an intellectual and perhaps even personal autobiography.

BIOGRAPHY:
SEEING A PERSON IN HIS HISTORICAL CONTEXT

Stone, Irving. *Those Who Love*. Garden City, N.Y.: Doubleday and Company, 1965.
   A fascinating book largely because of the author's meticulous research. The bibliography with its numerous sections shows clearly how seriously the author has taken the responsibility of conducting adequate research before writing a historical biography.

_____. *Lust For Life*. New York: David McKay Company, 1934.
   Stone bases his biography of Vincent van Gogh in large part on three volumes of letters that Vincent wrote to his brother Theo. While many might not want to follow Stone's technique of reconstructing scenes and dialogue based on what he came to know and understand about van Gogh, they would still find this technique worthy of study and consideration.

_____. *The President's Lady*. Garden City, N.Y.: Doubleday and Company, 1951.
   Once again, this book shows the basic technique that Irving Stone used in writing a historical biography. First he conducted extensive research consulting literally thousands of sources, both genealogical and historical. Then he interpreted the characters of his biography. Finally, he told their story recreating feelings, thoughts, and dialogue but making every effort to base that dialogue on individual, historical personality.

Tolles, Frederick Barnes. *George Logan of Philadelphia*. New York: Oxford University Press, 1953.
   Tolles's biography is based on original sources such as journals and letters. His claim is to see events through the subject's eyes, an interesting attempt to explore the historical perspective both of Logan and the period in which Logan lived. The writer of family history will find Logan a bit easier to relate to since he comes closer to describing the ancestor of a more common origin that most of us have.

Undsett, Sigrid. *Kristin Lavransdatter*. Translated by Charles Archer. New York: Alfred A. Knopf, 1969.
   This historical novel--the winner of the Nobel Prize in 1928--is the portrait of a woman of medieval Norway. While based on a great deal of historical research and understanding, it is not the result of genealogical research. What makes the book interesting for the family historian is the author's coupling of medieval dialogue and mindset to produce a story

that is at once historical, reasonable, and believable.

DIARIES AND JOURNALS:
WHAT MANY HAVE DARED THINK AND FEEL

Latham, Robert, ed. *The Illustrated Pepys: Extracts from the Diary.*
Berkeley and Los Angeles: University of California Press, 1978.
Little can be said to prepare the reader for the charm and surprising candor of Samuel Pepys's journal entries. While taking the time to detail the tragic fire of London of 1666 as well as even the most intimate sexual escapades of his life, Pepys provides the reader with a remarkable insight into the everyday life of a very secular, high public official during the mid-1600s in England.

Moulton, Phillips P., ed. *The Journal and Major Essays of John Woolman.* New York: Oxford University Press, 1971.
Woolman employs a remarkable spiritual sensitivity as he makes observations on slavery, simplicity in one's personal habits, and war that are far ahead of his time. His diary is an excellent record of the religious values that fired many Americans around the time of the Revolution.

Thomas, M. Halsey, ed. *The Diary of Samuel Sewall.* Vol I: 1674-1708. Vol. II: 1709-1729. New York: Farrar, Straus and Giroux, 1973.
Sewall's diary is filled with insights into the daily life of the Yankees of Boston, Massachusetts. While primarily famous as a member of the tribunal that presided over the famous Salem Witch Trials, Sewall left in his record enough references to secular interests, romantic love, and declining physical powers to allow the family narrator to capture a rounded portrait of a New England Puritan.

Woodforde, James. *The Diary of a Country Parson: 1758-1802.* Passages selected and edited by John Beresford. Oxford: Oxford University Press, 1978.
Largely preoccupied with the minutiae of food and drink, Woodforde gives us a record of the daily tedium of a country parson and his household and a record of the daily life probably typical of most English families during the latter portion of the eighteenth century. His diary captures the perspective of the socially secure Englishman who is more concerned with noises in his outbuildings than with the American Revolution, a stark contrast to the Sewall's and Woolman's records.

Wright, Louis B. and Marion Tinling, eds. *The Secret Diary of William Byrd of Westover, 1709-1712. Another Secret Diary of William Byrd of Westover for the Years 1739-1741.* Richmond: The Dietz Press, 1941.
Reminiscent of Pepys, Byrd, the founder and namer of Richmond, Virginia, kept a daily record of life on a colonial southern plantation a

half century before the American Revolution. While hardly a reflection
of life among the poorer classes of the South, it is still an excellent window into the thoughts of an eighteenth-century southerner.

THE ETHNIC AND IMMIGRANT FAMILY:
SURVIVAL IN AN ALIEN LAND

Bernstein, Burton. "Personal History of the Bernstein Family (Part I:
Sam and Jennie)," *The New Yorker*, March 22, 1982, 53-127, and
"Personal History of the Bernstein Family (Part II: The Kids)," *The
New Yorker*, March 29, 1982, 58-121.
Bernstein writes what is perhaps the classic family history, dividing
his narrative into two parts: the parents (Sam and Jennie), and the kids.
Focusing on what the term "family" meant in his personal case, he begins
with the historical, cultural, and ethnic background of each parent,
moving on to their immigration to the United States and their sharp personality differences. In the second part, "The Kids," he focuses on the
generation breach that divided the artistic and educated children, in
particular Leonard, from less-educated parents. He concludes by
returning to his basic theme, a definition of the Bernstein family, in a
meaningful summary. While the author avoids the controversial subject
matter of Joan Peyser's *Bernstein: A Biography*, his story comes as close
as any to what a family narrative should be.

Birmingham, Stephen. *"Our Crowd"--The Great Jewish Families of New
York*. New York: Harper & Row, 1967.
Birmingham narrates the climb to success of the socially elite Jewish
families of New York from 1837 through World War I. He marries the
individual family stories with national and international events, a technique that works well with families who find themselves at the very vortex
of these events.

Cather, Willa. *My Ántonia*. Boston: Houghton Mifflin Company, 1954.
Cather's chronicle is the story of a Bohemian woman's struggles
against both poverty and emotional tragedy. Her portrait of the members of an old-world family who cannot understand what is happening
about them and of a woman's determination to survive despite personal
mistakes and tragedy is moving. Time and age take their toll, and the
reader comes away with a deep faith in the ability of the human being to
adapt and maintain itself.

_____. *Shadows on the Rock*. New York: Alfred A. Knopf, 1970.
An interesting though not arresting story of a French family in early
Quebec. Basically a chronicle with little plot development, Cather's
story is a good example of a story that offers a warm, sensitive insight
into a family on the frontier but builds to no climactic conclusion.

Ferber, Edna. *So Big*. New York: Doubleday, Page, and Company, 1924.
    Basically a story of survival and determination, *So Big* is the story of a
young school teacher who marries into a Dutch immigrant family, is soon
widowed, and is left in charge of a vegetable farm near Chicago. She rears
a son who admires and yet rejects the rural values of his mother.

Moberg, Vilhelm. *The Emigrant Saga*: Vol. I, *The Emigrants*;   Vol. II,
    Unto a Good Land;   Vol. III, *The Settlers*;   Vol. IV, *Last Letter Home*.
    Translated by Gustaf Lannestock. New York: Warner Books, 1983.
    A moving and tender series of novels, this saga is the story of a young
married couple who with a group of people leave Sweden in 1850 to face
the sea, poverty and nature in Minnesota, the break with their former lives
in Sweden, and the final touching farewell to each other. Through detail
and plot focus, the author develops a story that gives the impression of
breadth and immense depth.

Roelvaag, O.E. *Giants in the Earth*. Translated by the author. New York:
    Harper and Brothers, 1927.
    Roelvaag's narrative is primarily a psychological characterization of
Beret, who because of her homesickness, cannot sink roots in a new and
hostile land. The novel is deficient in plot and is sometimes poorly told, but
it is a sensitive analysis of Norwegians who came to conquer and who were
in one sense conquered themselves.

Williams, Ben Ames. *Come Spring*. Camden, Maine: Down East Books,
    1968.
    Williams's novel about the settlement of Union, Maine, and the sur-
rounding countryside is based primarily on a diary as well as on other
genealogical and historical documents. Although the author takes considerable license in portraying the historical personalities, he has still produced
an excellent example of what a writer can do once he has immersed himself
in the local and genealogical history of a small community.

THE FAMILY NARRATIVE:
OVER ONE OR SEVERAL GENERATIONS

Bailey, Paul. *Polygamy Was Better Than Monotony*. Los Angeles:
    Westernlore Publishers, 1972.
    This charming family narrative combines local history (the Mormon
culture of American Fork, Utah) with family history to create a moving
story of inter-family conflict, parental incompatability, and childhood
rebellion. The book is both tender and humorous, but the author's main

achievement is to develop, through a few broad narrative strokes, a complete family portrait without resorting to the endless stringing of detailed trivia.

Egerton, John. *Generations: An American Family*. Lexington: University Press of Kentucky, 1983.
Centering his story on the two oldest-surviving members of one family, Egerton uses primarily oral sources to reach back several generations, and historical and genealogical sources to dramatize and personalize the more historically distant ancestors. Taking also "a few guesses" when there are gaps in the records, he creates through dialogue and oral history the illusion that he is talking his way back through the full nine generations and two and one-half centuries. This "metaphor for America" is useful for many reasons, perhaps the most important of which is the author's technique of having the deceased tell their own story.

Galsworthy, John. *The Forsyte Saga*. New York: Scribner, 1950.
Although Galsworthy wrote three trilogies chronicling the Forsyte family, this is the one worth reading. While supposedly the history of a family, the trilogy is actually a study of a class that for most of us holds no longer any great interest. Galsworthy's use of point of view, while not always clear, is of some value to the beginning family narrator.

Goldman, Peter, et al. *Newsweek: The American Dream*. New York: Newsweek, 1983.
Newsweek Magazine in this special anniversary issue focuses on Springfield, Ohio, and on five decades of five families. The families represent different classes and ethnic groups as well as immigrant arrivals and established Americans. The writers had access to oral histories as well as to countless historical documents to compile in five nonrelated families a composite story of America itself.

Grey, Zane. *Betty Zane*. Roslyn, N.Y.: Walter J. Black, 1933.
Grey's novel of the meeting and marriage of two of his ancestors is based on a diary and stories handed down in his family. It does not rank as a great novel largely because of its sentimentality although it contains vivid and arresting descriptions of life in the forest and on the frontier.

Haley, Alex. *Roots*. New York: Dell, 1974.
Basing his story on historical and genealogical research, Haley begins in 1750 with a family chronicle that covers seven generations of a black, originally slave family. Haley's story with its emphasis on dialogue and scene reconstruction is essentially a novel, and despite its immense popularity among family researchers, it is probably only a good model for that kind of writer who does not feel uncomfortable making guesses about the record.

Halter, Marek. *The Book of Abraham.* New York: Henry Holt and
 Company, 1986.
 Halter's two-millennial family history attempts too much and as a
result, fails to develop memorable characters and arresting plot conflict;
however, the book is a fascinating chronicle of a Jewish family if only because it provides the author the opportunity to tell the story of the
Jewish people in the Western world. While most family narrators would
find the book too much of a novel, they might find interesting the
author's technique of tying the complete, rambling story together with
the device of a mythical family record.

Keillor, Garrison. *Lake Wobegon Days.* New York: Viking Penguin,
 1985.
 Best known for his radio show "A Prairie Home Companion," Garrison Keillor combines almost microscopic detail with humor and rambling anecdote to tell his autobiography, the history of his small community, and the story of his family. While few beginning writers could
ever achieve Keillor's rare style, the book is a testimony to the range and
variety that the family narrative has shown in recent years.

Llewellyn, Richard. *How Green Was My Valley.* London: New English
 Library, 1984.
 A remarkably moving account of a Welsh coal-mining family that
struggles to maintain its cultural and emotional dignity amidst tremendous social change. One of its chief values for the family narrator is the
author's use of Welsh local color, culture, and dialect. There are three
other novels to the series: *Up, Into the Singing Mountain; Down Where
the Moon Is Small*; and *Green, Green My Valley Now.*

Mann, Thomas. *Buddenbrooks.* New York: Vintage Books, 1984.
 Mann tells the story of four generations of a wealthy northern German family. He takes the reader through the everyday events of a family
showing the gradual but inevitable decline of a family when its sense of
cultural destiny is destroyed by the onslaught of modern values.

Stegner, Wallace. *Recapitulation.* Garden City, N.Y.: Doubleday and
 Company, 1979.
 In many ways, this book is more appropriately categorized with the
autobiographies, but there are definite elements of family history. The
main character, on returning to his home town to attend a relative's
funeral, takes a mental journey through his life, a recapitulation. Stegner addresses so many local and family history themes that the book becomes the story of his family.

THE FAMILY-PROBLEM NARRATIVE:
THE TROUBLED FAMILY

Gray, Niguel. *Happy Families*. London: Futura Publications, 1985.
  While many will find this novel raw and offensive both in its subject matter and language, most readers will find the author's use of short scenes with flashbacks to childhood horrors an interesting technical device. Gray chronicles the destruction of human beings in a family characterized by emotional and mental sickness.

Hawthorne, Nathaniel. *The Scarlet Letter*. New York: W.W. Norton and Company, 1961.
  One of the great novels of all time, *The Scarlet Letter* is built around the issue of patrimony. Its emphasis on sin and guilt, while foreign to the modern reader, still captivate us by presenting an arena in which human beings struggle to deal with a reality that brings a family into existence as well with a sense of guilt that makes that family impossible.

James, Henry. *What Masie Knew*. Garden City, N.Y.: Doubleday and Company, 1936.
  Using the perspective of a young girl or as James himself phrases it "the ironic centre," the author describes the divorce of two parents and their ensuing chaotic world of lovers. A difficult book to read, it is interesting primarily for the way in which the author uses a young girl's point of view to tell a story.

Stegner, Wallace. *Angle of Repose*. Garden City, N.Y.: Doubleday and Company, 1971.
  A moving study of what we today define as the inability to communicate. In a plot that builds to a memorable and gripping resolution, Stegner chronicles the decline of a relationship through years of misunderstanding, reaching ultimately a tragedy that seals forever the gulf that divides the husband from the wife.

CHAPTER 2

USING GENEALOGICAL AND LOCAL HISTORY RECORDS TO WRITE THE HISTORICAL EXPOSITION

Many years ago some members of my family came to the imaginative conclusion that one of our ancestors--a certain James T. Worlton--had left behind in Bath, England, a rather considerable estate, a huge manor house or country estate, something on the order of Blenheim Palace. As the story ran, Worlton had generously placed the proceeds from the sale of this estate in the Perpetual Emigration Fund, which was then used to help poorer co-religionists leave England and settle in Utah during the mid 1800s. Actually Worlton himself had left the distinct impression that the property was certainly out-of-the-ordinary, describing the property as a court consisting of "a large house at the top of and six cottages on either side." As early as 1935, descendants of Worlton began to correspond with English relatives and city officials of Bath, but no one could offer any idea as to exactly what or where Timbrell's Court was or had been. The size and the value of the fabled ancestral estate grew, until some twenty years later two female descendants finally found the elusive "Court" and described their discovery in the following somewhat deflating words:

> Based on JTW's journal, some of the romantics of the family believed that this was our hereditary fortune, that this ancestral mansion with the cottages leading down the hill was something on the order of Chatsworth (a huge 18th century English manor house and country estate), and that we probably financed a dozen wagon

trains when all those proceeds were placed into the Perpetual
Emigration Fund instead of being saved for us. I must say that when
we saw Timbrell's Court, that idea began to evaporate...

(Noel Brusman, ed., *Worlton Family History*)

On a stone wall, they had indeed found the impressive words
"Timbrell's Court," but after picking their way through the debris--the
area had been bombed during World War II, they discovered that
Timbrell's Court had been anything but impressive. The so-called main
house had been a very average stone house adjoined by cottages whose
foundations indicated that they had themselves consisted of only two or
three rooms at the most.

Timbrell's Court is a good example of the hazards that await all
amateur family narrators. Seizing on words like "court" and "large
house," the inexperienced writer allows his fancy to overrule his sense of
judgment. Timbrell's Court is actually an impressive historical fact but
not for the reasons that Timbrell's descendants would have liked to have
it. "Courts" or "buildings" were a historical phase in English eighteenth-
century housing development projects. In fact, the term "court" describes
similar housing projects in American cities particularly in the building
boom after World War II. In the 1930s "courts" up and down England
fell victim to slum clearance projects and are today seldom seen. (See
W.G. Hoskins's discussion of "suburban growth and in-filling" in his
Local History in England.) Timbrell's Court is an excellent example of
suburban in-filling and suggests how a family history can be wedded to
local city history, in this case the history of Bath, England.

The problem is that most amateur family narrators and genealogists
are intimately familiar with the numerous books and articles that explain
in detail the sources of genealogical information, and publishers and
writers respond to this market by inundating us with articles and books
on vital records, census enumerations, probate and court records,
military records, and land records. Local genealogical organizations
with their endless seminars also focus primarily on sources and source
location. Most amateur family historians and genealogists emphasize
locating records, not analyzing them. Few seem interested in understanding how the family narrator can use sources to develop an accurate
and interesting family narrative. The result is an intellectual vacuum
that interprets speculative housing developments as palatial estates.

Few genealogists, amateur family historians, or beginning writers of
the family narrative take the time to understand either the local background or the general historical period about which they are writing.
One excellent book that addresses this problem is David E. Kyvig and
Myron A. Marty's *Nearby History* (Nashville: American Association for
State and Local History, 1984), which focuses on the analysis of local
history sources: published documents such as books, newspapers, direc-
tories, and maps; unpublished genealogical and family history sources;
oral documents; artifacts; landscapes and buildings; and visual docu-

ments such as photographs. The authors also, in their chapter "Linking the Particular and the Universal," address broader social and historical issues. An introductory approach is Frank Smith's *The Lives and Times of our English Ancestors* (Logan, Utah: Everton Publishers, Vol. I, 1974; Vol. II, 1980), an attempt to set forth the conditions under which our ancestors in England lived in the sixteenth through nineteenth centuries.

There is another problem that is related to the lack of preparation in historical background, and that is the tendency of most amateur writers to see family history as little more than the rearrangement of data from the family group sheet, a standard form used by genealogists to record information about a particular family. Consider the following student's history of John Farrow:

John Farrow was born in Dedham, Massachusetts, on November 6, 1776. He was the younger of two sons of Thomas and Elizabeth Farrow. John married Mary Oldfield, the daughter of Silas Oldfield and Hannah Dodge of Brookfield on January 14, 1802. Mary Oldfield was born on May 17, 1781, in Brookfield. John and Mary Farrow moved to Salisbury, Rutland County, Vermont, and their first son, Silas, was born there in 1803. The family returned to Massachusetts in 1808 and settled near New Salem in Hampshire County. John was a farmer and was listed as a grantor of land in New Salem records in 1823. Thomas, his brother, had married Lucy Oldfield in Brookfield in 1804, and he was listed as the grantee in 1823. Thomas later moved to Albany, New York, and opened a grocery store before 1820. John and Mary returned to Brookfield before 1820.

What has this history told us? Little that we could not have discovered by simply reading the family group sheet. What, for example, did it mean to be a farmer in New Salem in 1823? What did it mean to operate a grocery store? What was a grocery store? Why did John and Mary Farrow move to Vermont, and why did they return to Massachusetts? What does it mean to be a grantor of land or a grantee? It serves little purpose for the author to rearrange information from a family group sheet or a pedigree chart or to extract facts from a source document if he has nothing to add to the information or no point to make through organizing the information into a paragraph.

The family narrator must ask himself what the significance of the names, places, and dates was and see beyond the facts and dates to patterns or reasons. What was the occupational or financial background of the family? Were there any clear personality or psychological patterns? What was the relationship between the ethnic background of the family and its patterns of movement? Were there confessional or religious changes, and if so, why? And on a more personal and human level, what was the relationship of one historical character to another? Was there a weakness in a member of the family for which the others suffered or compensated? Were there misunderstandings that led to irreconcilable differences? Kyvig and Marty (*Nearby History*), in their chapter "What Can Be Done Nearby?" list scores of excellent questions that the writer should consider in interpreting original documents and writing family history: questions about the family (relationships, physical characteristics, location and movement, economics, daily living, education, military, and public affairs), places of residence (physical features, ownership, and use), neighborhood (physical and social features), organizations (general characteristics, business, education, culture, religion, and voluntary associations), community (physical, social, and economic characteristics; maintenance of order; health; and leadership and government), functional categories (environmental setting, economic activity, social relations, political affairs, and ideas and values). The authors present a similar series of questions in their book *Your Family History: A Handbook for Research and Writing* (Arlington Heights, Ill.: AHM Publishing, 1978). The beginning writer will find their specific questions very helpful. Other useful books, though more oriented to autobiography, are Patricia Ann Case, *How to Write Your Autobiography* (Santa Barbara: Woodbridge Press Publishing Co., 1977) and Jeanne W Pittman, *My Personal History Workbook* (Salt Lake City: Hawkes Publishing, 1979). Both of these books employ a chronological approach from early childhood through retirement.

After gathering facts then, the writer establishes reasons and motives behind the facts: in other words analyzes the source documents. Once this analysis is underway, the writer is in a position either to write a historical family exposition or to use his understanding to fashion a character sketch and to develop a plot--to tell a story or write a family narrative. The reasons and the motives--the patterns emerging from the facts--are limited only by the preparation and analytical ability of the writer, and the more the author understands the social and historical background connected with his subject, the more imaginative his approach will be, whether he is writing a historical family exposition or a family narrative. Since the possibilities are unlimited, the best way to start is to suggest some basic patterns and relationships that will help the beginning writer to analyze his own family; at least these patterns should serve as an inspiration leading the writer to develop other ways of looking at the facts that might more accurately explain his family.

WHERE DID THE FAMILY COME FROM AND WHERE AND WHY DID IT SETTLE?

The beginning point for almost every family narrative in the American setting is its ethnic origin. We are, after all, a nation of immigrants. Whatever the family has been or has become in America involves the country of origin and the cultural conflicts and resolutions that developed as a result of the family's settlement and migration pattern. Generally, they migrated with other families of similar national origin and often settled together in towns and communities in America. Settlers from the Old World transplanted the names of their towns of origin to the communities they founded in the New World. While many settled strictly along religious lines, many found the ethnic pull to be far more powerful. With the exception of the New Englanders who flocked to California during the Gold Rush, we are accustomed to thinking of religious dissidents settling together in the early communities of America. But the Welsh converts to Mormonism, for instance, found it far more comfortable to settle with other Welsh communities of Utah. They did not mix well with other early pioneers of the Salt Lake Valley, preferring instead the more familiar surroundings of the Welsh 15th and 16th wards (congregations) of Salt Lake City or the Welsh community of Malad, Idaho. Probably even among the Puritans, regional similarity was at least as important as religion when it came to settlement.

We often hear of the westward movement, but there were scores of regional movements within that broad category. The historical reality is that families, once they settled in the new republic, migrated in every direction imaginable. There were migrational patterns within states and local regions as well as along now-forgotten waterway routes. The Canal Museum in Syracuse, New York, contains over 900,000 manuscripts with references to "canal boat itineraries, survey maps, correspondence and bills of lading, newspaper clippings, passenger lists, bonds, manifests, time sheets and wage rolls, boat permits, damage claims, payrolls, land papers, lotteries, stock certificates, promises to pay and other records," all of which bear witness to the thousands who moved along the canal systems of the early United States. (See *The Source*, Salt Lake City: Ancestry Publishing, 1984.) A fact that few recognize is that even in Old World nations such as England, there have been clearly established migrational patterns stretching back to the Middle Ages. The English areas of Pembrokeshire in Wales attest to the practice of English-speaking populations settling together in foreign areas under English rule. (See W.G. Hoskins's discussion of urban development in his *Local History in England*.)

One document that throws light on the ethnic and cultural history of a family is the census enumeration. The first federal census enumeration to provide information on citizenship was the census of 1820: it had columns indicating whether the respondent was naturalized. State censuses also began about this time to provide columns on the citizenship and national origin of members of a family. The 1855 New York census, for example, provided a column for the number of years that each member of the family had resided in the city or town and two columns for designating whether the individual was naturalized or native. The 1850 federal enumeration provided information as to the place of birth; this was also the practice in the 1860 and 1870 enumerations. The 1880 and 1900 indicated the country of origin of the parents of the individual, the number of years the individual had been in the United States, and whether he had been naturalized.

However, knowing the ethnic origin of the family does not make it necessarily easy to understand the family's migrational and settlement pattern. The writer may be aware of the various moves that his German-Catholic family made, but he really needs to know what was happening generally if he is to understand why his family moved from one region to another. The movements of the Joseph Antoine Waller family is a good case in point. Both Joseph Antoine Waller and his wife Magdalena Dauer had been born in northeastern Alsace not far from each other; after marrying (probably in Alsace), they left France for Erie County, New York. But later this German-speaking Catholic family migrated to Wisconsin along the shore of Lake Michigan, then to Ste. Genevieve County, Missouri, and finally to Cullman, a small community north of Birmingham, Alabama. Instead of moving in a direct westward pattern, this family moved first towards the west, then southward eventually to the southern state of Alabama. The moves seem confusing and arbitrary. The family left no record that would give us any clue as to why it moved in such a pattern. Was it the attraction of the warmer climate? Was the family interested in the spoils of war after the close of the Civil War? Had the family formed southern sympathies while living in Missouri? Anything is a guess until the writer turns to a series of Census Bureau publications that summarize and analyze the census data. All of these publications are available on microfilm through most university libraries; for more complete bibliographical references, refer to *Bibliography and Reel Index: A Guide to the Microfilm Edition of United States Decennial Census Publications, 1790-1970.*

BUREAU OF CENSUS PUBLICATIONS:
CENSUS SUMMARIES

Return of Whole Number of Persons Within the Several Districts of the United States: 1790

Heads of Families--First Census of the United States: 1790

Return of Whole Number of Persons Within the Several Districts of the United States: 1800

Aggregate Amount of Each Description of Persons within the United States, and Territories: 1810

A Statement of Arts and Manufactures of the United States: 1810

Population Census for 1820

Digest of Accounts of Manufacturing Establishments in the United States, and of their Manufactures: 1820

Population, Fifth Census: 1830

Population, Abstract of Return of Fifth Census: 1830

Population, Sixth Census: 1840

Statistics of the United States of America: 1840

Compendium of the Inhabitants and Statistics of the United States: 1840
Census of Pensioners for Revolutionary or Military Services: 1840
Seventh Census of the United States: 1850
Mortality Statistics of the Seventh Census: 1850
Statistical View of the United States--Compendium of the Seventh Census: 1850
Message of the President of the United States, communicating a Digest of the Statistics of Manufacturers According to the Returns of the Seventh Census: 1850
Preliminary Report on the Eighth Census: 1860
Population of the United States in 1860
Manufactures of the United States in 1860
Agriculture of the United States in 1860
Population: Statistics of the United States in 1860
The Statistics of the Population of the United States: 1870 (Vol. I)
Vital Statistics of the United States: 1870 (Vol. II)
Occupations: Statistics of the Wealth and Industry of the United States: 1870 (Vol. III)
Population: A Compendium of the Ninth Census: 1870
Population: Statistical Atlas of the United States: 1870
Statistics of the Population of the United States: 1880 (Vol. I)
Statistics of Manufactures: Report on the Manufactures of the United States: 1880 (Vol. II)
Statistics of Agriculture: 1880 (Vol. III)
Report on the Agencies of Transportation in the United States at the Tenth Census: 1880 (Vol. IV)
Report on Cotton Production in the United States: 1880 Parts 1 (Vol. V) and 2 (Vol. VI)
Report on Valuation, Taxation, and Public Indebtedness in the United States at the Tenth Census: 1880 (Vol. VII)
Report on Valuation, Taxation, and Public Indebtedness in the United States: 1860 (Vol. VIII)
Report on the Forests of North America: 1880 (Vol. IX)
Production, Technology, and Uses of Petroleum and its Products: 1880 (Vol. X)
Vital Statistics - Report on Mortality and Vital Statistics of the United States at the Tenth Census: 1880 Parts 1 (Vol. XI) and 2 (Vol. XII)
Mines and Quarries - Statistics and Technology of the Precious Metals (Vol. XIII)
Mines and Quarries - U.S. Mining Laws and Regulations Thereunder, and State and Territorial Mining Laws (Vol. XIV)
Mines and Quarries - Report on the Mining Industries of the United States (Exclusive of the Precious Metals) (Vol. XV)
Manufactures - Reports of the Water-Power of the United States Parts 1 (Vol. XVI) and 2 (Vol. XVII)
Statistics of States and Cities - Report of the Social Statistics of Cities: 1880 Parts 1 (Vol. XVIII) and 2 (Vol. XIX)

Report on the Statistics of Wages in the Manufacturing Industries, with Supplementary Reports on Average Retail Prices of Necessaries of Life, and on Trade Societies, and Strikes and Lockouts (Vol. XX)

Report on the Defective, Dependent, and Delinquent Classes of the Population of the United States as Returned at the Tenth Census (Vol. XXI)

Report on Power and Machinery Employed in Manufactures, Embracing Statistics of Steam and Water Power Used in Manufactures of Iron and Steel Machine Tools and Woodworking Machinery, Wool and Silk Machinery (Vol. XXII)

Compendium of the Tenth Census Parts 1 and 2

A Report on the Oyster Industry of the United States: 1880

Report on Population of the United States at the Eleventh Census: 1890 Parts 1 and 2 (Vol. I)

Report on the Insane, Feeble-Minded, Deaf and Blind in the United States at the Eleventh Census: 1890 (Vol. II)

Report on Crime, Pauperism, and Benevolence in the United States at the Eleventh Census: 1890 Parts 1 and 2 (Vol. III)

Report on Vital and Social Statistics in the United States at the Eleventh Census: 1890 Parts 1, 2, 3, and 4 (Vol. IV)

Agriculture; Irrigation; Fisheries--Eleventh Census: 1890 (Vol. V)

Report on Manufacturing Industries in the United States at the Eleventh Census: 1890 Parts 1, 2, and 3 (Vol. VI)

Report on Mineral Industries in the United States at the Eleventh Census: 1890 (Vol. VII)

Report on Population and Resources of Alaska at the Eleventh Census: 1890 (Vol. VIII)

Report on Statistics of Churches in the United States at the Eleventh Census: 1890 (Vol. IX)

Report on Indians Taxed and Indians not Taxed in the United States (except Alaska) at the Eleventh Census: 1890 (Vol. X)

Report on Insurance Business in the United States at the Eleventh Census: 1890 Parts 1 and 2 (Vol. XI)

Report on Real Estate Mortgages in the United States at the Eleventh Census: 1890 (Vol. XII)

Report on Farms and Homes: Proprietorship and Indebtedness in the United States at the Eleventh Census: 1890 (Vol. XIII)

Report on Transportation Business in the United States at the Eleventh Census: 1890 Parts 1 and 2 (Vol. XIV)

Report on Wealth, Debt, and Taxation at the Eleventh Census: 1890 Parts 1 and 2 (Vol. XV)

Compendium of the Eleventh Census: 1890 (Vol. XVI: Part 1, "Population," Part 2, "Vital and Social Statistics: Educational and Church Statistics; Wealth, Debt and Taxation; Mineral Industries; Insurance; Foreign Born Population; Manufactures," and Part 3, "Population; Agriculture; Manufactures; Fisheries; Transportation; Wealth, Debt and Taxation; Real Estate Mortgages; Farms and

Homes; Indians")
Abstract of the Eleventh Census: 1890
Statistical Atlas of the United States Based Upon Results of the Eleventh Census: 1880
Vital Statistics of Boston and Philadelphia Covering a Period of Six Years Ending May 31, 1890
Vital Statistics of District of Columbia and Baltimore Covering a Period of Six Years Ending May 31, 1890
Vital Statistics of New York City and Brooklyn Covering a Period of Six Years Ending May 31, 1890
Report on Social Statistics of Cities in the United States at the Eleventh Census: 1890
Eastern Band of Cherokees of North Carolina

The Bureau of Census publication *The Statistics of the Population of the United States: 1870* provides a plausible explanation of why the Joseph Antoine Waller family moved in such a puzzling pattern. The first clue is in the "German Population" map on page 326 of the publication, which shows the relative density of German-speaking Americans in the eastern half of the United States in 1870. According to this map, there were over fifteen Germans per square mile in 1870 in the Erie County area, fifteen Germans per square mile in the Wisconsin area, and fifteen Germans per square mile in the Ste. Genevieve area; only in the isolated German-speaking community north of Birmingham--Cullman--does the count per square mile drop below six. Obviously, The Waller family preferred German-speaking communities to more culturally assimilated areas. When we consider Table XVIII, "Statistics of Churches," pp. 528-60, of the same publication, we understand why the Waller family chose these particular German-speaking communities. The table on page 546 lists eleven total churches in Ste. Genevieve County with 2900 sittings. Of the eleven churches, six are Roman Catholic. The Joseph Antoine Waller family was German-speaking Catholic (Alsatian), and judging from the following excerpt from a letter that the family received in 1853 from their family in France, they treated matters of religion with seriousness: "Have your children educated and do not forget God; offer a child to the Lord, as it is from God." The moves made by the family were probably motivated both by a desire to be near German-speaking Americans as well as by a desire to be near Roman-Catholic Germans, no doubt Alsatians from their particular corner of Alsace.

Late in life, probably in 1880, Joseph and his wife left Farmington, St. Francois County, Missouri, for Cullman, Alabama, a small German-speaking community some forty miles north of Birmingham, Alabama. It had been fifty years since Joseph Antoine Waller had married Magdalena Dauer in Alsace and relocated with her to Erie County, New

York. Their sense of Alsatian cultural identity had remained strong through all these years, and in their old age both Joseph and Magdalena probably again felt its pull. They had migrated across the eastern and midwestern portions of the United States leaving their children behind to form their own now culturally assimilated families. Now in their advanced years, they still wanted to live in a German-speaking community. While neither Joseph nor Magdalena left behind a record of this last move, one of Joseph's grandchildren wrote in a letter that both Joseph and Magdalena had not cared for the German community of Cullman and had decided to continue on to Birmingham. It took fifty years for the couple to make the transition from Alsace, France, to the United States; and both husband and wife finally did so only a few years before they died. The census publications proved to be invaluable in understanding the cultural attitudes of this family. By carefully considering the facts and the possible motives behind the facts, we were able to see a pattern that could eventually become a fascinating story about an obscure but unique immigrant family that over a century ago made the long, difficult transition from a foreign culture to an American culture.

The bibliographies at the close of each of the sections in this chapter--in this case the section discussing family origin and settlement patterns--move from interpretations that are more objective and easily verified to those that are subjective and somewhat tentative. (These bibliographies are analytical and also highly selective; the assignment of items to each bibliography is in many cases arbitrary, as most works could just as easily fit under several headings. The writer should turn to Chapter 4: "Point of View" for bibliographies of background works.) As we move from the public aspect inward to the personal life of the individual and family, we increasingly draw conclusions or make interpretations that are much more open to debate. Even though our objective data decreases, we proceed having the confidence that our interpretations are justified because we have built on the foundation of what has gone before. However, each writer must decide for himself the point beyond which he cannot proceed, the point at which nonfiction becomes fiction; the writer of fiction, obviously, will find all conclusions the legitimate basis for narratives.

BIBLIOGRAPHY: FAMILY ORIGIN AND SETTLEMENT PATTERNS

Unruh, John David, Jr. *The Plains Across: The Overland Emigrants and the Trans-Mississippi West, 1840-60.* Urbana: University of Illinois Press, 1982.

A well-researched study of the antebellum pioneers who crossed the plains. This imaginative and comprehensive book lays to rest many old myths and stereotypes by getting at the truth and the reality of the westward migration. Includes an extensive bibliography of primary and secondary sources.

World Conference on Records: Preserving Our Heritage, August 12-15, 1980.

Vol. 3. *North American Family and Local History, Part 1:* Burke, Frank G., "308: The Americanization of the 'New' Immigrants in Utah"; Vecoli, Rudolph J., "316: Documenting the Lives of European Emigrants to North America"; Jonasson, Eric, "321: The Families of Western Canada: Their Immigration and Multicultural Background"; Anderson, Robert Charles, "324: Migration and Settlement Patterns in Colonial New England."

Vol. 4. *North American Family and Local History, Part 2:* Harriss, Helen L., "350: The American Melting Pot: Ethnic Backgrounds and Family History (A Case Study of Western Pennsylvania)"; Pritzkau, Gwen, "369: Pioneers on Two Continents: Germans tRussia and America"; Smith, Clifford Neal, "361: Why American Families Migrated"; Swierenga, Robert P., "357: The Anatomy of Migration: From Europe to the U.S. in the Nineteenth Century"; Ybarra-Soriano, Lea, "354: Chicano Families in the United States."

Vol. 7. *Continental European Family and Local History:* Law, Hugh T., "507: Overcoming Barriers to Genealogical Research in Belgium"; Smelser, Ronald M., "506: Germany Is As Close As Salt Lake City: The German Microfilm Collection of the Genealogical Society."

Vol. 8: *Scandinavian Family and Local History:* Naeseth, Gerhard B., "606: Norwegian Immigrant Churches."

Vol. 9. *Latin-American and Iberian Family and Local History:* Johnson, Ann H., "703: Migration, the Individual, and the Family in Latin America: A Historical Perspective"; Modell, John, "703: Migration, the Individual, and the Family in Latin America: A Historical Perspective."

Vol. 10. *Australasian and Polynesian Family and Local History:* Cross, D.J., "810: Immigration and Colonial Settlement in Australia and New Zealand: Bond and Free"; Gunson, W. Niel, "811: Early Migrations and Settlements in the Pacific Islands and the Nature of Inter-Island Relationships"; Morris, Robert J., "815: The Crossroads of the Pacific: The Development of Multicultural Families in Hawaii."

Vol. 12. *Historical Change in Population, Family, and Community:* Lees, Lynn Hollen, "208: Migration to the City in Modern Europe"; Lehning, James, "206: Immigration and the Family"; Modell, John, "204: Mobility and Industrialization."

HOW DID THE FAMILY EARN ITS MONEY AND HOW DID IT SPEND IT?

After cultural and religious motivation, the main reason people left the Old World for the New was probably money; and once securely established in the New World, people continued to give the matter of financial well-being top priority. It was a consideration in marriage, migration, and basic life-style decisions. In any narrative, it is a matter that the writer cannot afford to ignore; it can be a dominant theme, or it can simply be a matter of background interest. But it is always part of the story.

The Worlton Family of Bath, England, the owners of the fabled Timbrell's Court, was a family of shoemakers or cordwainers although earlier members of the family had been involved in carpentry and land speculation. For most of us the shoemaking trade has little romantic appeal. Despite the fact that the Worlton Family had some meager wealth or was at least self-sufficient, Worlton family histories have consistently passed over the shoemaking aspect of the family. Much of this neglect is because of the original Worlton journal, which emphasizes Worlton's religious activities and his migration to Utah. However, there is no reason why subsequent family narrators should have avoided an aspect of the story that is as fascinating as the religious aspect: Worlton's part in the economic life of Bath, England. Most of us are familiar with the novels of Jane Austen who depicted the endless social whirl of Bath, its world of dresses, balls, and Beau Nash. But what were the economic factors that gave rise to this world, and what about the army of dressmakers and, yes, shoemakers that made it possible? How did they live, how much money did they make, and what kind of social status did they enjoy? R.S. Neale in his exhaustive study of Bath, *Bath: A Social History 1680-1850 or A Valley of Pleasure, yet a Sink of Iniquity*, explores in detail the wage-earning classes, and no family history that purports to tell the story of a shoemaking family in Bath, or England for that matter, is complete without considering it. In Worlton's case, there is a journal, and there are sufficient historical studies to make the task a fairly easy one; but what about the obscure ancestor that has left little more than a few clues?

The probate document is often an excellent source of clues about a person's or a family's economic standing. The inventory, when included in probate documents, lists the value of each item in the possession of the deceased. The probate documents relating to the estate of John Dauer (probated in 1872) detail the amount of the property in John Dauer's possession; there is also an accounting of the notes that he held against other persons as well as notes others held against his estate. The probate papers also provide the final amount distributed and the actual amount that John Dauer was worth at the time of death: $848.94. Obviously John Dauer was a man of moderate means at the time of his death. If we turn to the 1855 New York census, we learn that John

Dauer some ten years before his death owned some sixty acres, valued at $1200, indicating that in his later years he was probably worth around $1000.

A similar document for a certain Elisha Partridge who died in 1787 in Maine gives his estate at death as valued at 300 pounds, 6 shillings, and 2 pennies with debts of exactly 198 pounds and 18 shillings against the estate. The total value is of great importance in writing about the financial state of the Partridge family as it is in the case of John Dauer, but in both cases the inventory reveals far more than simply the total assets at death. Consider the inventory of John Dauer's property listed below. When read from left to right, the items are listed probably in the order in which the man who made the inventory moved through the house:

Inventory of John Dauer's Property

one cow	one cow	two tables
two iron wages	one saw	one cook stove
one fanning mill	one stand	one bureau
one overcoat	coat and jacket	looking glass
one bedstead	six chairs	one rocker
one rocker	one feather bed	one feather bed
two pillows	two quilts	one comforter
two quilts	two bags	three pair pants
one pair pants	one coat	two pair boots
three pictures	one cap	one hat
five sheets	two pillow cases	four shirts
four towels	two flannel shirts	

If we divide the items into specific areas, we conclude that he first noted the items outside the house, probably in the barn or some kind of outbuilding: two cows, two tables, two iron wages, and one saw. Then he moved to the kitchen area of the house noting the cook stove and the fanning mill. And finally to the sleeping area: stand, bureau, looking glass, bedstead, chairs, rockers, feather beds, quilts and pillows, and articles of clothing. It would appear from the inventory that John Dauer and his wife lived in a two-room house with a humble outbuilding or barn. Using the same technique, we turn now to the inventory of Elisha Partridge who died some hundred years before:

Inventory of Elisha Partridge's Property

a gray wrapper and straight bodied blue coat
blue jacket and grey straight bodied coat
stripped jacket and brown linen coat
leather breeches and linen diaper jacket
linen and wool shirts and an old beaver hat

a pair of blue and white stockings
blue leggins and one pair of old shoes
linen breeches
silver knee buckles and silver shoe buttons
one Bible and church platform
tobacco box
sheep shearers and chopping knife
toasting iron and iron lamp
Dr. Watts Psalms
Dr. Watts Hymns with four other sermon books
15 spools and two shuttles
two reeds, one 40 at yard and one 26 at yard
pair of temples and tin lantern
brass warming pan and skimmer
plemes and pair of spectacles
razors, hone, strap, and lather box
jackknife, gimlets, and awls
hammer and pinchers, spring and staple
sickles and shovel and tongs
wooden funnel and cider keg
tea kettle and piggens
flax comb and one old gray wig
iron hayhook and wooden mortar and pestle
pewter plates and pint basins
pewter dishes and table spoons
knives and forks and butcher knives
pewter dish and pair of shearers
tin tea pot and pair of steelyards
gun, bayonet and powder horn
lead inkstand and pair of woolcards
iron pot and baskets
clove basket, meal chest, and cupboard
pigeon net and iron trammels
earthen pots and old tray and great chair
small box, water pail and flour barrels
barrel, dye pot, and white mug
coverlids
bed, bedstead and bedding
sole leather and hogsheads
scythes, stone nibs and wedges with rings
meal sacks, bobsled, and chopping axes
100 pounds of pork and meat barrel
sheep's bell, meal sack and valet of cups and saucers
white chest
fish and barrel and ten sheep
calf skin, yearling, and one pair of steers
one cow and hog

grass scythe and log chain
flax in the stack
Indian corn and bushel of peas
flax
washing tubs and foot wheel
wool, hoe and 34 bushels of potatoes
5 bushels of turnips and one bushel of wheat
pitch fork

The items can be roughly grouped into the following categories: clothing; books and tobacco box; sheep shearers, chopping knife, toasting iron, and iron lamp; weaving equipment; cooking implements mingled with shaving tools, jackknife, gimlets, flax comb, and gray wig; eating utensils; gun, bayonet, and powder horn; inkstand and woolcards; large pots, chests, baskets, cupboard, nets, barrels, mug, and chair; bed and bedding; farming implements; grains and food with livestock; and dishes. Confusing as this list is, there is a certain logic to the items. It is obvious, first, that the one who took the inventory began inside the house, moving generally from clothing to weaving equipment to cooking implements to eating utensils to larger food containers to chair and finally to bed and bedding. Then he must have moved outside the house to consider the farming implements, grains, livestock, and flax. The total estate must have been composed of a one-room house and one or more small barns or outbuildings.

Inventories are valuable tools for gaining an insight into exactly how a family lived even two centuries ago. Certainly, the writer will want to check his conclusions with contemporary descriptions of living quarters and homes, but here we have an excellent beginning, almost literally gaining entrance to the home and living standard of two families that lived up to two centuries ago.

Land records are another indicator of economic wealth, and in Joseph Antoine Waller's case they provide a running historical picture of his financial holdings. In 1841, Joseph and Magdalena Waller sold a lot in the City of Buffalo, New York, for the sum of $600. In 1848, they purchased a piece of property for $350. Then in 1860, they purchased 360 acres in Missouri for $800, in 1865 eighty more acres for $200, and in 1868 eighty additional acres for $150. Apparently all of these pieces of property were contiguous so that by 1868--the date of his father-in-law John Dauer's death--Joseph Antoine Waller owned 520 acres for which he had, over a period of eight years, paid approximately $1200. In other words, Joseph Antoine Waller held ten times as many acres as his father-in-law, who had owned only sixty acres, although the actual value of each farm was apparently similar: Dauer's sixty acres were valued at $1200 in 1855, the same value placed on Waller's 520 acres by totaling his expenditures made from 1860 to 1868. From 1875 through 1883, Joseph began to sell off portions of his comparatively large holdings for a total amount of $2100, retaining a portion for himself. Many of these transactions were with close relatives, so it is difficult to determine exactly what the true value of the property was. Assuming that he sold the parcels at their true market value, the original investment had almost doubled in value over a period of approximately twenty-five years. The picture becomes more complete when we turn to the census enumeration.

Starting in 1850, the United States federal census began to provide information on the financial condition of the family (column 8 gives the value of real estate). The 1860 enumeration expanded this to include information both on real and personal estate, and with the 1900 census, there was information on the family's home--whether it was owned or rented, free-titled or mortgaged, a farm or a house, and whether there was a farm schedule. Certain states began to provide similar information at about the same time. The 1855 New York census, for example, provided detailed information on the acres worked, the cash value of the property, the tools and implements, and the various products produced. Starting around 1850, the writer of the family narrative is able to gain through the census enumerations significant insights into the financial history of a family. When entries were made for Joseph Antoine Waller and his family in the 1870 census, the enumerator gave Joseph's occupation as farmer and his total real estate value as $2500. While I cannot account exactly for the discrepancy between the figures of $2100 in 1883 and $2500 in 1870, I cannot help but believe that a landholder would instinctively undervalue his real estate to a federal enumerator. I do feel confident that the figures are close enough to be reasonably accurate especially when one considers that the parcel that Joseph held back for himself probably represented the amount missing in the figure of $2100 for 1883.

Once again, a Bureau of Census publication (see the previous list of census summaries), in this case the volume entitled *Occupations: Statistics of the Wealth and Industry of the United States: 1870* (Vol. III), gives us a valuable yardstick for evaluating both the deed and census information. The following list gives the breakdown for farms in Ste. Genevieve County, Missouri:

700 Total Farms

1 farm under 3 acres
21 farms from 3 to 9 acres
77 farms from 10 to 19 acres
220 farms from 20 to 49 acres
229 farms from 50 to 99 acres
80 farms from 100 to 499 acres
1 farm from 500 to 999 acres
1 farm over 1000 acres

Land in this particular section of Ste. Genevieve County, Missouri, costs at today's prices between $300 and $550 per acre--much of the land in this area is hilly, rocky, and not tillable--while land in Eden, Erie County, New York, where Joseph's father-in-law held his sixty acres, costs around $500 per acre. There is some uncertainty as to the exact size of Joseph Antoine Waller's landholdings in Missouri, but it would appear that Joseph owned one of the largest farms in the county (approximately 520 acres), if not the second to largest farm, and that farm probably afforded him some level of financial security and comfort. When we think of a person living out the American promise--owning property and continually improving himself--we have to think of Joseph Antoine Waller, the immigrant from Alsace, France, who "made good."

Economic wealth, then, becomes a measure of many things. At the most superficial level, it is an indicator of a person's monetary value, but it is also a subtle indicator of life-style. Items from a probate inventory tell us not only what a person owned but probably also how he lived, such as the conveniences or luxuries he owned and enjoyed as well as the number of rooms in his house and its likely size. And a person's monetary worth gives us additional clues as to what a person could buy and enjoy. We have all spent hours thumbing through old mail-order catalogues amazed at how inexpensive items used to be. The 1902 *Sears, Roebuck Catalogue*, a reprint edition, gives us some indication as to the cost of goods about twenty years after Joseph Antoine Waller sold his land in Missouri and thirty years after John Dauer died in Erie County, New York. One could buy a man's suit for about $5, a pair of shoes for $2, a buggy for $25 to $75, a plow for $5, and a stove for $15 to $25.

It is difficult to establish standard of living in 1870 by comparing 1902 prices with prices of similar items today (prices had also dropped in 1902 approximately one-third from their 1870 level), but one can contrast the relative value of land in 1870 with the value of similar land today. John Dauer's sixty acres at today's prices would run about $30,000, a very modest estate; Joseph Antoine Waller's 520 acres would cost between $156,000 and $234,000, the lower figure being probably the accurate one. Even without taking into account the value of land, it is possible to conclude on the basis of size that John Dauer's total assets in 1870 were modest indeed, although sixty acres in 1870 were probably sufficient to provide the basic needs of a family. Most farms in the New York state census of 1855 were about sixty acres, exactly the size of John Dauer's farm. Taking size as a measure, his son-in-law, Joseph Antoine Waller, seemed to stand a good deal higher on the social scale as one of the largest landowners in Ste. Genevieve County. Also, although the relative value of land today in Erie County and Ste. Genevieve County on a per acre cost basis is roughly similar (about $500 per acre for tillable land), land per acre undoubtedly cost more in 1870 in Erie County than it did in Ste. Genevieve County where it was more heavily wooded. Total assets do not translate into spending power; one's personal value system has as much to do with what one buys as does his capacity to buy.

But, if we accept the size of each piece of property, the value of land in today's prices, and the 1902 edition of the *Sears, Roebuck Catalogue* as any kind of general guide, both men were probably very typical of the thousands of farmers who lived in the eastern and midwestern regions of the United States in the late nineteenth century.

BIBLIOGRAPHY: HOW THE FAMILY MADE AND SPENT MONEY

Braudel, Fernand. *Civilization and Capitalism, 15th-18th Century.* Vol. I: *The Structures of Everyday Life.* Translated and revised by Sian Reynolds. New York: Harper & Row, 1981.
The author focuses on the themes of everyday life--demography, food, costume, lodging, technology, money, and towns--to define the context in which pre-industrial economies operated.

Greven, Philip J., Jr. *Four Generations: Population, Land, and Family in Colonial Andover, Massachusetts.* Ithaca: Cornell University Press, 1970
The author analyzes the genealogical histories of twenty-eight separate families and their relationship to the land, delineating over four generations the familial changes that resulted from changing economic and demographic circumstances.

Neale, R.S. *Bath 1680-1850: A Social History or A Valley of Pleasure, Yet a Sink of Iniquity.* London: Routledge and Kegan Paul, 1981.
The author emphasizes the economic aspect of social history, giving a very comprehensive picture of what it meant to work and live in Bath in the seventeenth and eighteenth centuries.

Pitt-Rivers, Julian Alfred. *The People of the Sierra.* Chicago: The University of Chicago Press, 1961.
While this book primarily examines the social structure of a Spanish-Andalusian village, it does focus in several chapters on agriculture, industry, and trade.

Powell, Sumner Chilton. *Puritan Village.* Middletown, Conn.: Wesleyan University Press, 1963.
Powell explores the interplay between the "three distinct types of English experience"--the open-field village, the English borough, and the East Anglican village--and the formation of the town of Sudbury, Massachusetts.

Tolles, Frederick Barnes. *Meeting House and Counting House: The Quaker Merchants of Colonial Philadelphia, 1682-1763*. New York: W.W. Norton, 1948/1963.

The author explores the Quaker value system and the relationship between that system and Quaker economic, social, and intellectual life between 1682 and 1763.

Wilson, Charles. *England's Apprenticeship: 1603-1763*. New York: St. Martin's Press, 1965.

A social history of the time when commercial enterprise in alliance with state power changed the old English agrarian economy from "the Manor of England" to "the workshop of the world."

WHAT DID THE FAMILY
CONSIDER IMPORTANT OR VALUABLE?

Where people settle and how they spend money as well as what they do and say are reflections of their values. Individuals normally value what their culture or society indicates they should value although we all know how individual value systems can pull against social and cultural value systems. A modern, technically-oriented America may value production and assign rewards to the man or occupation that produces the largest quantity and best quality of goods, but a so-called "free spirit" could decide that he prefers writing poetry and collecting welfare and thus reject the dominant value system of his culture. A more traditional, religiously-oriented society may value commitment to the church, expecting a father and mother to dedicate one of their sons to the priesthood, while the son growing up in nineteenth-century America may value financial wealth and have the personal wherewithal to implement his independent value system. The writer of family literature has a twofold task: he must determine what the value system of the culture or society was or is at the time of his narrative, and he must determine, if he can, the value system of his individual subject or family. Much of the material for a good story lies exactly in how or to what degree the individual or family value system compares or contrasts with the value system held by the larger society or culture.

A person's native culture and religious orientation have an important influence on his value system. John Dauer and Joseph Antoine Waller, both natives of Alsace, were practicing Roman Catholics, although it would appear that religion was more important to John than it was to Joseph. When John died, he died within the womb of mother church. His son-in-law, Joseph had a much different relationship with Roman Catholicism. In 1853, Joseph corresponded with his relatives in Alsace, and one letter from relatives in France has survived. It reveals a concern on the part of the family in Alsace as to Joseph's and his family's orthodoxy. As quoted earlier, the family directed Joseph to educate his children—presumably in the church—and to dedicate one of his sons to the church, a standard practice among rural Catholics of this time. This may have been simply standard advice to someone living so far from home and in such a wild and untutored land, but this concern was well grounded. Most of Joseph's children eventually married outside the faith, and Joseph and his wife seemed to leave cultural orthodoxy increasingly behind as they migrated farther and farther from Erie County, New York. A century earlier, Elisha Partridge's probate papers included in the inventory a list of religious books. It is well established that the Puritans of New England valued education, particularly religious education, as a means of eluding the "Old Deluder," and Elisha Partridge as a member of a family that had its roots in Dedham, Massachusetts was certainly in that tradition. In the three cases— John Dauer, Joseph Antoine Waller, and Elisha Partridge—it appears that religion was valued though it is difficult to determine exactly how much.

Education is another important value. Elisha's probate papers indicate that he valued education. He had several books in his possession although as I have stated above they were exclusively religious: a Bible, a church platform, hymnals, sermon books, and a collection of psalms. But Elisha also had an inkstand among his last effects indicating that not only could he read but he probably also could write. As mentioned above, this was probably a result of his Puritan heritage, but it is still an insight into Elisha Partridge's value system. It is interesting to contrast Elisha's educational level with many of the early Welsh immigrants who came to the United States around 1850. Most were illiterate—compulsory education did not begin in England and Wales until 1870—and could only make a mark when their signature was required, indicating that education in early nineteenth-century Wales did not reach down to the lower classes. In the families that we have been following—the Dauers, Wallers, and Trapps—we can observe some interesting patterns as to education. The New York state census of 1855 shows clearly that both John and Selma Dauer, the first-generation immigrants from Alsace, could read and write and that their children of ages thirteen and eleven were in school in 1850 (according to the federal census) while the children of their closest neighbors were not. The Waller children seemed to enter school as soon as they were old enough. Their two oldest daughters, Catharine and Barbara, were in school when nine and seven respectively (again, according to the 1850 federal census). Twenty years later, all of their minor children—both boys and girls—were still in school although those apparently over eighteen years no longer attended (according to the 1870 Federal Census). From both censuses, we learn their neighbors' children generally attended school although there were many cases in which some and indeed all of the children had not attended school within that year. As for the Trapps, the third generation, the 1880 federal census records that the oldest son of seven had not attended school during that year, although the 1900 federal census records that all in the Trapp family could read and write, and that the children ages fifteen, twelve, and nine attended school eight out of twelve months while the oldest daughter of nineteen was not in school and one son of seventeen was a farm hand. It was common for the children of the Trapps' neighbors to attend school. It would be safe to conclude that for this family, all three generations, education was valued, although a seven-year-old son did not attend school for one year. Years later, this son's sister remarked to her niece that Christian Trapp had changed jobs so many times that it was difficult for the children to attend or finish school. Even though education was valued, other factors made it difficult for the children to be educated at all times. Through the census returns and other documents such as probate papers, it is easy for the writer to determine whether eduation is a personal, family, or cultural value.

There is also the value of change, the absence of stability. It is well established that movement or change was so much a part of American life that it became itself an American value. There have always been migrational changes even in the Old World, but perhaps at no time in the history of mankind has change itself occurred with such regularity and rapidity. The reason for a change probably no longer mattered. As Nicholas Perkin Hardeman indicates in *Wilderness Calling*, Frederick Jackson Turner's "safety valve" theory was not corroborated by the migrational patterns of his family. "Not depressed conditions, but success seems to be positively related with the frontierward impulse" (*Wilderness Calling*).I suspect that people moved not because they had either been successful or wanted to be more successful, but because change itself had become an established value. The experiences of many of the families we have considered seem to support both Hardeman's conclusion and the idea that being American meant changing one's locality periodically. In 1840, we find the Joseph Antoine Waller family in New York, then in Canada, again in New York in 1851, by 1860 in Wisconsin, by 1870 in Missouri, and by the mid-1880s in Alabama. At no time does this Waller family move because of economic plight; rather Joseph buys and sells land much as if buying and selling were itself a value. Probably opportunity did beckon. Wisconsin did offer land opportunities in the 1870s; but the moves to Missouri and then to Alabama seem to have been made more from the desire to move on than from any desire to become more successful. Indeed, the last move took Joseph and his wife away from most of their family to a relatively new area; in Birmingham Joseph bought two small houses, one of which he rented out and one in which he lived, a typical American retirement move. For Joseph Antoine Waller change itself was a value. The John Dauer family provides a stark contrast. Apparently John Dauer did not share his son-in-law's interest in change. From the time John and his wife Selma disembarked in New York, around 1832, stablity was their primary value. They built up a farm in Erie County and made only minor moves--there is one move from Boston Township to Eden Township, which seems to have occurred when John retired from active farming: as with Joseph Antoine Waller, he divested himself of his land holdings, but he made no move across several states to retire. He remained as he had always been, a simple but stable farmer.

Sociologists have established that a great deal can be deduced about a family and what it values through its choice of living-room furniture. (See Edward O. Laumann and James S. House, "Living Room Styles and Social Attributes: The Patterning of Material Artifacts in a Modern Urban Community," *The Logic of Social Hierarchies*, edited by Edward o. Laumann et al., Chicago: Markham Publishing, 1970.) Most of us are instinctively aware of the subtle differences in the placement of the television set. The family that has a television in each bedroom and one squarely in the center of the living room probably would have little in common with the family that places its only television in the family room or even more discreetly behind cabinet doors in the game room. Soviet families or families emerging from a very traditional cultural context tell a lot about what they value when they center their refrigerators in the living room. The inventory of the probate document offers the nearest thing to a listing of the furniture in a frontier American home, and while the inventory from Elisha Partridge's probate documents (1787) does not reveal much as to style or period of furniture, probably meaningless questions anyway, it does indicate, through a general listing of possessions, a great deal about the value system of the deceased and his wife. This becomes especially apparent when we contrast John Dauer's inventory with Elisha Partridge's.

When John Dauer died in 1868, he left behind four pair of pants, a coat, two pairs of boots, two vests, four shirts, one cap, one hat, and two flannel shirts, a limited but useful wardrobe for a man who had once been a farmer and who had spent the years before his death semi-retired. When Elisha Partridge died in 1787, almost 100 years before, he left behind a much more impressive wardrobe (see the previous list). The mere quantity as well as the variety of articles in Elisha's wardrobe--especially when one considers that Elisha preceded John Dauer by almost a century--contrasts sharply with the simplicity of John's wardrobe. There is an item in Elisha's inventory that deserves a special note: "one old grey wig." During the Colonial Period, there was a good deal of shifting in attitudes about which class could legitimately wear a wig and some ambivalence later in the same period about the wearing of wigs. Samuel Sewall, on Tuesday, 10 June 1701, records in his diary that he visited Josiah Willard to call him to repentance for the wearing of a wig while according to John Miller, "the Reverend Cotton Mather appeared before his congregation in a periwig. Among the upper class, the fashion was embraced eagerly; a wig became 'de riguer' and no gentleman would be seen without one in public. In the towns, even children and servants wore them. With the passage of time, wigs became increasingly elaborate and expensive." (John Miller, *The First Frontier: Life in Colonial America*, Lanham, Md.: University Press of America, 1986.) When one considers Elisha's taste penchant for silver buckles and silver buttons as well as for wigs, we are tempted to conclude that Elisha's style of dress reflected town rather than farm values and perhaps also a movement toward a higher social class. If John Miller's statement describes local values in Union, Maine in 1787, it is obvious that Elisha Partridge did not dress as a farmer. It is tempting to assume that Elisha either attended events or frequented places where wigs and silver buckles and buttons were considered appropriate and that he was a more socially aware personality than the rather simple and frugal John Dauer. But these are matters for the next section.

BIBLIOGRAPHY: VALUES

Boyer, Paul and Stephen Nissenbaum. *Salem Possessed: The Social Origins of Witchcraft*. Cambridge, Mass.: Harvard University Press, 1974
An exploration of the interaction between the ordinary men, women, and children of Salem Village; the institutions of the town; and the witchcraft trauma of 1692.

Frost, J. William. *The Quaker Family in Colonial America*. New York: St. Martin's Press, 1973.
This book is a definition of the Quaker faith, an analysis of Quaker family life, and a description of Quaker family life covering the period from 1672 until the American Revolution.

Miller, John C. *The First Frontier: Life in Colonial America*. New York: Dell, 1966.
A re-creation of the ways in which the American colonists lived: how they courted, married, reared children, educated themselves, ate and drank, engaged in sports and recreations, dressed, worshipped, punished crimes, and engaged in slavery.

Stone, Lawrence. *The Family, Sex and Marriage In England, 1500-1800*. New York: Harper & Row, 1977.
This massive book analyzes and explains the shifts in value systems in England from 1500 to 1800, which were expressed in the ways members of the family thought about, treated, and related to each other.

Zuckerman, Michael. *Peaceable Kingdoms: New England Towns in the Eighteenth Century*. New York: Knopf, 1970.
This book is a scholarly and somewhat difficult-to-read study of the

system for the keeping of peace in the eighteenth-century Massachusetts town.

WHAT KIND OF SOCIAL STANDING AND PERSONALITY PATTERNS DID THE FAMILY EXHIBIT?

A family or any individual member of the family is always closely related to the craft or occupation of the males of the family. This is particularly true of a traditional culture such as nineteenth-century America and is true even today despite the increasing role of women in the market place. And the occupational or the professional level is related to the income level, the educational background, the social status, and probably even to the personality and emotional stability of the family.

While statistical studies of the occupational prestige of earlier centuries are obviously impractical if not impossible, there have been numerous attempts to rank occupations since World War II. Pineo and Porter's national study of occupational prestige for Canada ranks professionals such as lawyers, high government officials, country court judges, and university professors at the higher end of the scale; semiprofessionals such as pilots and nurses somewhat lower; farmers and small business managers lower than semiprofessionals; and unskilled laborers at the low end of the scale (Peter C. Pineo and John Porter, "Occupational Prestige in Canada," *The Logic of Social Hierarchies*). Richard Centers, in the article "Class Consciousness and Class Structure" *(The Logic of Social Hierarchies)*, points out that in most people's minds "the upper and middle classes comprise mainly the business and professional people" although "the position given to farmers is, in contrast, the most ambiguous of all, for considerable percentages of all four classes--upper, middle, working, and lower--name them as members." Obviously, there is a real difference between "farm owners and managers, farm tenants, and farm laborers."

What about the class system of nineteenth-century America? Starting with the census of 1820, enumerators began to ask for information about males engaged in agriculture, commerce, and manufacturing. The census of 1840 identified the number of persons in a family that were employed in mining, agriculture, commerce, manufacturing and trade, navigation of the ocean, navigation of canals, lakes and rivers, and learned professions and engineering. With the 1850 census, we have the nominal census for the first time, and the enumerators began to ask the respondents to name the profession, occupation, or trade to which they belonged. The census of 1850 set the pattern for the next five censuses.

It is obvious from the questions being asked by the census enumerator that an occupational shift was taking place as well as a shift in people's attitudes as to which occupations or professions they held in high and low esteem. In the 1820 census there was no mention of the so-called professional. America was a nation of agriculture, commerce, and some manufacturing. In 1840 the terms "learned professions and engineering" appear for the first time, and by the time of the 1850 census, "profession" heads the list, followed by "occupation" and "trade." If position on a list is telling, it would appear that professions were in some kind of priority position. The writer should consult the publications of the Bureau of the Census if he wants to explore this issue more completely.

Someone involved in agriculture during the nineteenth century, a farmer like Joseph Antoine Waller, was probably ranked, as Centers suggests, either as upper, middle, working, or lower class on the basis of land ownership and size of land held. In the period following the Civil War, the Anglo-Saxon upper class seems to be in a dominant social position although it seems probable that possession of land, considerable amounts of money, education, and title such as military rank in themselves also figured in the equation. Since Waller was a first-generation, German-speaking immigrant who held no title and had little education, his possession of the second-largest farm in Ste. Genevieve County probably counted for relatively little. Socially, Waller probably belonged to what we could describe as the middle or working class.

There is, however, much more to this matter than the occupational or social stratification of one member or one generation of the family. Through the census, the family narrator cannot only identify the occupational or professional background of individual members of a family, but he can trace the occupational or professional history of the family. Both John Dauer and his son-in-law Joseph Antoine Waller—first generation Americans— engaged in farming in Alsace as well as in the United States, but when both families begin raising children in the United States, their second-generation American males begin to leave farming for occupations such as carpentry and commerce. The change, however, is only one of form not substance, for they still engage in what we would see as middle or working class occupations. Subsequent history shows little evidence of "learned professions" such as engineering or any indication of upward mobility. The family that starts off as farming middle or working class in the nineteenth century continues to be occupationally middle class through at least three generations. Participating in the so-called American dream may have meant for both the Dauers and the Wallers more material assets and greater personal fulfillment, but it did not mean much social mobility.

The personality of a historical figure is a bit harder to establish, but once again there are definite clues in the documents. A young German immigrant named Christian Trapp left clues about his personality in various genealogical records. Christian first appeared in the United States in 1872. One year later, he married Joseph Antoine Waller's daughter, Magdalena Waller, in St. Louis, Missouri. His obituary of some thirty-five years later gives his occupation as that of a brewer, a trade that he followed "all of his life." The obituary further states that Christian had learned the trade in the "old country," having held "responsible positions in the breweries of Germany, Russia and France before he came to America" (*The Standard*, Butte, Montana, 14 January 1908). First stopping in New York City, he later came west "to the brewery centers of Cincinnati and St. Louis, working as head brewer in the principal breweries of those towns." Jerry Mahoney, a fellow worker had the following glowing report about Christian Trapp:

> You cannot say too much good about him. He was a good man in every sense of the word and there were few men in the United States who were better at his profession. Every man about the brewery was his friend and all over town he has friends who will regret the news of his death.

The problem is that contemporary records from St. Louis do not warrant a positive reaction much less bear out the contention of the article that Trapp worked as head brewer.

The St. Louis City Directory of 1873 does list Christian Trapp's occupation as that of a brewer; however, the city directory of 1874 gives his occupation as a driver, the 1875 directory as a laborer. Admittedly there could well have been more than one Christian Trapp in St. Louis, but there is too much evidence that all three references are to the same Christian Trapp, the man who years later is reputed to have been the head brewer in the principal breweries of Cincinnati and St. Louis. Besides the discrepancy, there is the disturbing fact that Christian Trapp seemed to change jobs often, at least once a year when he lived in St. Louis. In 1880, the U.S. federal census gives Christian's occupation as "cooper" or barrel maker; even though probably still associated with the brewery business, Christian was in 1880 most likely employed at still another job. The fact is that Christian Trapp's employment record would indicate to a modern personnel director that this is a man who is for one reason or the other unstable. Certainly, few companies today would want to hire a man who appears to change jobs at least once a year. While many would object to such a bold interpretation, the record seems clearly to bear out that Trapp's personality interfered in some way with his job, probably because of a bad temper or because of basic incompetence. The latter interpretation is a bit unfair as Trapp did seem to be familiar with the brewery business; he certainly remained associated with breweries all his life. Years later, one of his daughters, in a private conversation with her niece, revealed that Trapp's children never went to school a full year because Christian Trapp would get into an argument or fight with someone at his work and have to look for a new job. What about Mahoney's report and the fact that in later years Trapp did remain for eight years with the Butte Brewing Company? Probably Christian Trapp simply did learn as he grew older to get along better with his co-workers, but the fact is that the record clearly leads us to conclude that when he was younger, his personality for one reason or the other made it difficult for him to hold a job much longer than a year.

Probate documents are another source of social standing and personality patterns. The inventory of the real and personal estate of Elisha Partridge (see the previous list) includes, among other things, the following items: sheep shearers, chopping knives, spools and shuttles, giblets, hammer, pinches, hayhook, mortar and pestle, gun, bayonet, powder horn, pigeon net, iron trammels, scythes, nibs and wedges, fish and barrel, sheep, yearling, steers, cow, hog, log chain, flax, corn, wool, hoe, potatoes, turnips, wheat, pitch fork, and two hundred acres of land in Thomaston, Maine. Elisha Partridge was clearly a self-sufficient landowner. In a period of American history when agriculture was the primary function of almost all Americans, Elisha resembled most other middle or working class landholders in Maine. Certainly he was not a scholar, a man of commerce, a minister, a large landowner, a professional bureaucrat, or local military leader. He was probably very similar to the vast numbers of self-sufficient yeomen farmers that lived on the Maine frontier around the time of the Revolution.

When Elisha Partridge died in 1787, he had notes against his estate to the sum of about 64 pounds, most apparently incurred as a result of long-standing obligations. His total assets in personal property ran at around 67 pounds; he also owned 200 acres of land valued at 80 pounds and held notes against two other parties valued at 140 pounds. Others held two long-standing notes against his estate totaling 160 pounds. For reasons that are not clear, these were not paid at the time of the settlement of the estate. In terms of actual cash then, Elisha Partridge had debts at the time of his death totaling 227 pounds while he possessed about 207 pounds (excluding the value of the 200 acres). Excluding property, Elisha owed more than he owned. If one takes his property into account, he died with a positive cash value of 60 pounds; but he had claims against 75 percent of his total estate. Today one would describe this as living very much on the margin. According to John Miller, however, "an American farmer could hardly avoid going into debt. Since the outlay required for the purchase of land and farm implements often exceeded an individual's resources of cash, he was obliged to borrow-- usually from the local storekeeper." Farming has always been a demanding and credit-prone operation, but when John Dauer died a century later, his probate papers gave a much different account. John had notes against his estate totaling about $26 while he held notes against others totaling about $762. When he died, there were claims against his estate of only 3 percent of the total assets. Even if we accept John Miller's arguments about the Colonial farmer and take into account different historical and social conditions, we cannot avoid making some kind of personality analysis of both John Dauer and Elisha Partridge. That one died with money in the bank and that the other died deeply in debt seems to indicate that the first was far more conservative and circumspect about money and resources than the second. We will return to this matter later, but it is interesting to note that the inventories of both reveal a fairly simple and frugal John Dauer and a somewhat more stylish Elisha Partridge, which could explain why one died with money in the bank and the other died heavily in debt.

It is both fascinating and dangerous to jump to conclusions about the personality of a man who lived two hundred or even one hundred years ago. We have referred often to Elisha Partridge, each time on the basis of some historical or genealogical document. Up to this point we have not attempted to show Elisha Partridge as a character in a story. Several years ago, Ben Ames Williams wrote *Come Spring*, a novel about a small Maine town called Union, and, in this novel, Elisha Partridge is a minor character with a very distinct personality. Williams based his novel on Sibley's *History of Union*, which, while furnishing the basic outline of the novel, in no way furnishes the kinds of personality details that Williams attributed to Elisha Partridge. In fact, there is really no record that allows us to see Elisha Partridge as the raw, over-sexed bore that Williams's novel depicts him as:

> Partridge proved to be a man as old as Philip Robbins, or even--Mima thought--a little older; a full-blooded, fat man with purple cheeks and a way of laughing soundlessly till his face became congested with blood. Mrs. Partridge was a buxom young woman as merry as he. They welcomed Joel and Mima robustly, and Mrs. Partridge said:
> "I hear you two are just married yourselves. 'Lish and me got together three years ago." She chuckled merrily. "The old goat was bound he'd have me, one way or another, and I decided I might as well marry him as have to sue him for the baby's keep. I didn't waste a minute. Lucky, too. Baby came on the dot of nine months. Alibeus, his name. Ain't he a chubby young one?" Alibeus was chewing contentedly on a crust of cornbread, sitting on the floor; and Mrs. Partridge shook all over with mirth to watch him and added: "I'm due to let go in September."
> Her husband roared with appreciative laughter and slapped her backside soundingly. "Hurry it up, Sal," he said. "Make room for another passenger. A man my age can't waste time!"
>
> (Ben Ames Williams, *Come Spring*)

This obviously is the work of a writer who has made a huge jump from the record to the narration. While no one would argue that Elisha Partridge could well have been the kind of individual depicted here, all would agree that the historical record does not support such a personality description.

BIBLIOGRAPHY: SOCIAL AND PERSONALITY PATTERNS

Demos, John. *A Little Commonwealth: Family Life in Plymouth Colony.* New York: Oxford University Press, 1970.
    Basing his analysis on artifacts, wills, inventories, and legal documents, the author reconstructs the ordinary social life of the family in Plymouth Colony.

Emmison, Frederick George. *Elizabethan Life: Disorder.* Chelmsford: Essex County Council, 1970.
    This volume deals primarily with felonies committed in Essex during the latter part of the sixteenth century.

_____. *Elizabethan Life: Wills of Essex Gentry and Merchants.* Chelmsford: Essex County Council. 1978.
    A collection of wills arranged by class and occupation.

James, Mervyn. *Family, Lineage, and Civil Society: A Study of Society, Politics, and Mentality in the Durham Region, 1500-1640.* Oxford: Clarendon Press, 1974.
    A study of the basic structural--social, political, and attitudinal--differences between sixteenth- and seventeenth-century Durham, England, as seen in the shift from lineage to civil society.

Laslett, Peter. *Family Life and Illicit Love in Earlier Generations.* Cambridge: Cambridge University Press, 1977.
    This book is a historical sociology focusing on that segment of society that over succeeding generations exhibits a tendency towards illegitimacy.

Riesman, David. *The Lonely Crowd: A Study of the Changing American Character.* New Haven: Yale University Press, 1950.
    An analysis of the so-called, modern American type or the character of the individual "other-directed" member of the "new Middle class."

Roberts, Robert. *The Classic Slum.* Manchester: The University Press, 1971.
    An analysis of the domestic lives of the Edwardian poor.

FROM THESIS TO HISTORY:
THE TECHNIQUES OF EXPOSITION

The first step in writing a historical family exposition is to develop a workable thesis; throughout this chapter we have done little else except consider potential theses and to suggest avenues of developing other theses through a consideration of the facts. Once the writer has a thesis that he feels the facts will support, he is in a position to outline the basic format of his exposition. The thesis can be broad, relating to the general history of a family, or it can be very narrow, relating specifically to one man or to one period in a man's life. It is simply a matter of what the facts will support and how long the final product will be. If I wanted to show that the Dauer and Waller families exhibited a gradual but perceptible improvement economically, a movement from lower middle class to upper middle class, I would need to devote several pages to the supporting facts and conclusions to be drawn. If, however, I were to establish that Christian Trapp's occupational history was characterized by instability, it would probably require only a long paragraph. As mentioned above, it is a matter of available details and of how much detail I would personally want to use in writing the exposition. Remember, the thesis must always establish or prove something about the subject. To write generally about Christian Trapp is not to frame a workable thesis; such would result in a paper that could include information about his family and marriage as well as about his jobs. To write more specifically about his occupational history would also not be workable since I could include information about the breweries he worked at as well as about his occupational instability. I must instead frame a thesis that is so specific and so directing that I cannot stray in presenting supporting detail. One workable thesis would be to establish that Christian Trapp's personality led to his losing job after job. This thesis would allow me to admit only those facts that prove one specific point. Otherwise, I would simply wander from point to point providing information about Christian Trapp but never establishing or proving a thesis.

While the function of the thesis is always to prove or establish, there are different kinds or types of theses and thus different ways in which the writer establishes or proves his point. If I want to show simply that Trapp was very unstable, I could provide a series of *examples* in which this was true. Perhaps I want to show how Christian Trapp went about losing his jobs, in other words the *process*. In this case I would show the steps he went through in acquiring and losing his jobs. I could *define* the particular version of occupational instability that Christian Trapp exhibited. I could *compare or contrast* Christian Trapp with his eldest son who seemed to be very stable occupationally. Or I could *classify* the various kinds of ways in which he lost his jobs: those in which he lost his temper, those in which he was incompetent, and those in which he lost interest. I could show the relationship between his personality and his loss of employment (*causal analysis*). Many consider description a different type of writing separate and distinct from either narration or exposition, but both exposition and narration use description to advance their own purposes. For our purposes then, we will consider it now as a type of exposition. If I chose to describe Christian Trapp as he appears in an old photograph, I could employ description to make a basic point about the subject. Each of these calls for a different kind of thesis statement and for a different kind of organization.

The next step is to frame an outline. Placing the thesis at the top of the outline, I would proceed to delineate exactly how, for example, I plan to classify the ways in which he lost his job. If the history is limited by detail, I might consider three support paragraphs, one dealing with his temper and the loss of employment, the second dealing with his lack of ability and the loss of employment, and the final dealing with his short attention span and the loss of employment. If I have more details at my disposal, I might consider several paragraphs for each point. However, I build at all times to a final concluding statement or paragraph in which I restate the thesis and make some final observation. The success of a good exposition depends on the care with which the writer frames his thesis, develops his outline, and provides good detail as support.

Let us now consider two of these expository types: description and example. Professional writers of exposition such as MacFarlane in his *The Family Life of Ralph Josselin* and Bennett in his *The Pastons and Their England* employ all of the expository types listed above, namely: example, classification, causal analysis, definition, process, and comparison and contrast. The amateur writer of family exposition, however, is probably mainly interested in either description or example.

Description. Description, although it does not fit neatly into the category of exposition, has one basic thing in common with all exposition: it begins from a basic thesis or idea. There are many details that occur to you, but you have some basic thing that you want to establish about the subject. The following description based on two photographs of a writer's parents does mix some direct exposition with actual description. Consider how she builds each description around a basic idea--for her father the basic idea is that of a chained dandy or to use her metaphor "tethered hawk," and for her mother the basic idea is the hardened disciplinarian. Consider how she uses details that support those basic ideas. I have italicized and underlined the basic idea of each description and italicized only the description details:

> I do not know these people in the old photographs who are my immediate ancestors, my parents: James Anthony Myrick and Rose Anderle Myrick.
> By the time I knew the elegant *dandy* in black and white, he was older, heavier, more weather-and-life-worn. Can this be the once-boy described to me by an elderly relative as "my favorite cousin . . . *wild as a hawk*, that one." Surely not the roistering lumberjack of

the north woods who gave it all up for love's sweet sake when he met the perfect lady shown on the other photograph. He just might have been the high-salaried sawyer in a mill, the aristocracy of the business . . . $5.00 a day, imagine . . . or he might have been (although he looks too young) already the owner of three sawmills in three different Wisconsin and Michigan cities. The *wild hawk tethered in dark suit and stiff, white-bosomed shirt and high collar, with black bow tie. The curly black hair that I remember is disciplined straight, except for a hint of rebellion at the edges.* Actually, he was the "fun" parent, the one we saw all too seldom, but when he was home brought with him an aura of laughter.

Neither do I recognize the pictured young woman as the mother I, the youngest of four, knew. *Oh, she stayed stylish under all circumstances and the face was round, but the trusting look and innocence of that face and eyes had vanished.* She had learned the vicissitudes as well as the joys of life. She had married a hard-drinking, hard-working, hard-playing young man and had borne five children, one of whom died in infancy. She had washed and ironed and cleaned and cooked and sewn and raised her children. The short, curly hair could be today's fashion, but not the dress, with its tight bodice and waist and stiff skirt. I wonder if it could be made of bombazine, the material so often described in books of that period, which I learn from a just-consulted dictionary is a "fine-twilled fabric, usually with silk or artificial silk warp and worsted filling." She was the *disciplinarian*, she had to be because the father of her children would not or could not be. It was only as I matured that I learned to love her as much as I did my wild Irish Dad.

(Violet Hester)

Each detail of the descriptions--the stiff shirt, the straight hair, the tight bodice, even the material of the dress--supports the basic ideas and build to the concluding statement that the author may not have found her mother as much fun as her dad, but she did learn to love her as well.

Example. Example is the most basic and most easily controlled form of exposition, and it is the basis of all the other forms of expository writing: the writer backs up a generalization, an abstract assertion, with a specific example. Like description, it proceeds from a basic thesis or idea: something that the author is proving or establishing about the subject. As in description, the detail must be vivid and above all directly related to the thesis. The author must not introduce any detail that is not connected to the thesis; otherwise, the paper will wander. The following student exposition states the thesis at the end of a somewhat lengthy introduction: "Sadly, Grandma Redman had been in her grave many years before I learned to appreciate what a courageous, indomitable little lady she actually had been." Then the paragraphs that follow, in one way or the other, are or contain examples of the subject's unconquerable courage. Normally each support paragraph begins with a topic sentence, itself a minor thesis sentence, which states the basic idea of the support paragraph but in turn supports the basic idea of the entire paper. The writer intersperses many of the example paragraphs with historical transitions that help set the background as well as lead the reader from one support paragraph to the next support paragraph. Finally, there is the conclusion with the thesis restated. There is a basic weakness in that there is a certain overlap in the last two support ideas: "Margaret kept her farm and her family functioning" and "For Margaret money was still a nagging problem." This aside, the paper works well as an example exposition. I have italicized the thesis sentence, the topic sentences, and the final concluding statement so that the technique is clear:

My Pioneer Grandmother,
Margaret Friday Redman

[Introduction:]

One of my early childhood memories is of a little woman in a long, white nightgown and mobcap kneeling at a bedside, her hands folded in prayer. My maternal grandmother, on a rare visit to our home, had been given the room that my sister and I normally shared. Heedlessly, I opened the door, intent upon retrieving some forgotten personal item. After one startled glimpse of Grandma, I closed the door and hastily retreated, aghast at my blunder.

I remember other occasions when, after promising a visit, Grandma did not come. The whole family would stand on the depot platform as a gigantic railroad engine shrieked and rumbled straight toward us, finally screeching to an earthshaking halt not more than a yard away. Clinging to my father, I would watch carefully as each passenger descended--but no Grandma.

As the train rumbled on into the night, Father would herd us back into the car, and we would make our way homeward, anxiety a palpable presence in our midst. Tense with worry, Mother would give the telephone operator the number of her brother or sister from whose home Grandma had written. The reply to her anxious query was always the same--Grandma had changed her mind! Mother would go absolutely limp with relief, while Father grumbled about inconsiderate people.

To my shy, childish mind, Grandmother Redman was an awesome, willful, distant little lady, not at all like my other grandma, who bestowed smiles and hugs and told fascinating stories. It was not until years later that I finally understood my mother's plaintive remark, "I wish you could have known my mother when she was really herself." *Sadly, Grandma Redman had been in her grave many years before I learned to appreciate what a courageous, indomitable little lady she actually had been.*

[Support Paragraphs:]

Born in a Wisconsin log cabin, *Margaret Marie Henrietta Friday was, above all else, a survivor.* Her German immigrant parents bore twelve children, only seven of whom lived beyond childhood. The second child born, Margaret was the first to thrive. In 1871, at age eighteen, she became the bride of Michael Carl Redman, Jr., an immigrant German farm hand who had managed to save two hundred dollars out of his wages.

[Now follows a series of transitions and support paragraphs that move the reader through a number of important points mainly setting the historical background and making the point that life on the frontier could be extremely difficult.]

Margaret clung to the land and her home. She owned one eighty-acre plot of land clear, but she was in danger of losing her home place. In 1895 her brother, H.P. Friday of Markesan, Wisconsin, acting for their father George Friday, obtained title to the home eighty at "sheriff's sale" for the sum of $726.65 and reconveyed it to his sister Margaret. Two years later, upon the death of their father, this amount was deducted from Margaret's share of the estate, as he had instructed in his will. Since the inheritance had to be divided nine ways, this accounted for most of Margaret's share.

Somehow, despite money worries, hard work and the cruel vicissitudes of the prairie weather, Margaret kept her farm and her family functioning. Rose continued to live at home for six years while teaching school. Her brother Albert declared that his sister Rose was the best teacher he ever had. According to my mother, Rose also made most of the clothes for the younger members of the family. Clara and Laura went out to work as household helpers for other farm families and, before long, married. George and Albert took over the operation of the farm. But the prairie continued to be a fierce adversary. There were more bad years than good.

This summer, Roy Smith, a cousin of my mother's, recalled that as a small boy he traveled with his mother from his home in Wisconsin to visit my grandmother. He described her farm in one word--"bleak."

Finally, at the turn of the century, Margaret made a big decision. She bought a house in Albee and moved her family there, renting out the farmland. There is evidence that she received some sort of financial help for this venture from Will Roberts, her sister Louise's husband. To support her family she rented out rooms. In the 1900 census there is a listing of "Maggie Redman, age 47, occupation landlady, house owned free of mortgage." Four subteen children were still at home, plus faithful Rose, George, and Albert.

Continually haunted by money problems, Margaret finally sold the farm to daughter Marie and her husband, who owned adjoining land. They cultivated the land but had no need for the house. For years the old house and barn stood vacant and forlorn, sad reminders of things that had been, or might have been.

My mother remembers that while she was still at home, her mother boarded teachers. When school was out for the summer, Margaret rented a house at Big Stone Lake, and some of the teachers moved there with her for their summer vacation. Mother was afraid of the water and hated that summer at the lake.

[Now a transition paragraph in which the writer describes the children leaving home.]

For Margaret money was still a nagging problem, so she rented out the whole downstairs of her house and lived upstairs. At another time, she rented out the whole house, except for one room to store her furniture and moved in with her son George and his wife in the town of Milbank, nine miles away. But life was by no means grim. Distances did not destroy the family's affection for one another, and several of the children had remained close by. Some of my cousins fondly remember large family Thanksgivings and Christmases at Grandma's house in Albee, when the table would groan with good things to eat, brought by sons and daughters who lived nearby.

In 1918, with some financial help from her children, Grandma sold the Albee house and bought a home near son George in Milbank. There, too, she rented out rooms. In addition, the eleven children worked out an arrangement whereby they all contributed to her support. When she was no longer able to care for herself, that house, too, was sold. It was then that Grandma began visiting around at the scattered homes of her children in Dakota, Minnesota, and Iowa. She was beginning to be childish and forgetful.

[Conclusion:]

In her later years, Grandma's eleven children and their families gathered annually, on the weekend nearest her birthday, for a family reunion on the lawn at Uncle George's house in Milbank. Even Aunt Anna, who lived in far-off Florida, would be there. Each year a commercial photographer was hired to memorialize the occasion. Grandma would be seated on the lawn in a rocking chair, with the family members lined up on either side and behind her. The photographer used an odd sort of camera that slowly moved from one end of the group to the other, resulting in a picture so long that it would not fit into an album; it had to be rolled up for storage. I have one of those group pictures showing a smiling Grandma, with nearly fifty family members gathered around her.

The out-of-staters on these occasions were bedded down at the various local aunts' and cousins' homes. I remember my family being housed at Cousin Graycie's farm home, on land that had once belonged to Grandpa Michael and Grandma.

What fun those reunions were! Always bashful at first, in record time my cousins and I would be playing together like long-time friends. I squirmed a bit as aunts and uncles "made over me." And Grandma? She was just that dignified little white-haired lady that we all gathered around to have our pictures taken.

Finally, in Grandma's declining years, the reunions stopped. Cousin Graycie cared for her in her home. It was there, in 1934, that Grandma died, at the age of eighty-two. She was buried in the Milbank cemetery, and Grandpa Michael's and little Benjie's remains were moved there from the Reville cemetery, to rest beside her.

In her eighty-two years, Margaret Friday Redman achieved no widely heralded great deeds. Nonetheless, her contribution to the world was significant. Through good times and bad she stood firm, giving life to, loving and nurturing eleven good, moral men and women. *She met the harsh prairie on its own terms, refused to be defeated by it, co-existed with it.*

No Mother, as a child I didn't really know her. But through learning of the circumstances of her life and times, I feel that I know her now, and I count it a privilege. She was a gallant lady.

(Naomi Hooper)

The technique is relatively simple. In the opening paragraphs, you state clearly what you plan to establish; then you provide examples which establish that basic point; and finally you restate what you set out to establish. Now let us consider another expository technique: the process paper.

Process. In writing a process paper, the author shows how something happened--the steps of the actual process. In the following exposition, the writer employs details that she gleaned from a series of calendars and makes the basic point that the family decision to leave the farm was a gradual one. First in the opening paragraph she presents her basic thesis then provides some background material about the war years and the demands of farm life. In succeeding support paragraphs, she presents each main step in the process of leaving the farm. At the end of the paper, she restates her thesis in a concluding series of statements. Once again, I have italicized the basic theme or thesis of the process paper, each basic step or main idea of each supporting paragraph, and the concluding statement:

In compiling the information derived from these calendars, the problem was to describe farm building and farm life in such a way as to be true to the material and also to use the disconnected series of happenings which were recorded in an attempt to write a coherent history. Every page has a story or two hidden in sparse line of comment about people, events, and situations. There is no plot, no characterization, no progression of action into another except that of seasonal growth. But there is a theme. The calendars touched on the war years and farm development, but *the underlying theme of these years was a gradual series of moves away from the family farm*.

War in Europe began August 1, 1914, and while President Wilson declared United States's neutrality on August 4, 1914, it was impossible not to be affected by those early war years. Three times a week the ten-mile round trip on horseback was made to the Paradise post office to pick up the mail. Sometimes George's young sons would go; sometimes he or Harve would go, bringing the news of the world to the neighborhood. An entry on April 3, 1917 stated, "Read the news." Diplomatic relations with Germany had been broken off on February 3, and war was declared on April 6. On April 7, the same terse line, "Read the news." The calendars record how much activity was generated by this declaration. Liberty loan bonds and war saving stamps were bought; Red Cross units were formed. Sweaters and mufflers were knitted using yarn supplied by the Red Cross. Children learned to knit and cut squares for gun wipes. Rationing went into effect. Sugar was rationed 5 pounds at a time. George's eight-year-old son reminded the hired man, "one spoonful, Volley."

Heavy snow and late freezes delayed spring planting in 1917. The stock with the new calves and colts had to be rounded up from the canyons and fed from the hay stacks. This weather was followed by the longest dry spell ever experienced in the area and resulted in smokey and dirty air caused by forest fires. Because of the severe drought, the grain crops were poor and fruit and garden produce was not plentiful. In addition to this, the stockmen were concerned about cattle rustlers, one of whom had been killed. The commission houses in Portland sent buyers of cattle and grain into the community. Prices of farm products were good. The drought and hail had destroyed some crops, but insurance helped lessen the loss.

The same day that war broke out in Europe, May 1, 1914, Grandma Reavis died. *This was the beginning of a series of changes for the Hendrickson family*. George's son, Clayton, had gone to school in Enterprise since 1908 while living with his grandmother. He spent the summers on the farm in Paradise. It seemed wise now for the family to begin to think about moving to Enterprise for the school year. The Reavis house was remodeled with the addition of two upstairs bedrooms and an inside toilet. The three older children lived there with a caretaker family while attending school and eventually all the family moved there during the school year, frequently going back and forth to Paradise. In the summer, the children's friends visited on the farm.

The second change that eventually resulted in the family's leaving the farm was that George's health gradually worsened; so on July 5, 1917, George and Nellie went to Portland to consult a nerve specialist, Dr. William House. They were gone eight days. George was no longer able to do heavy work at 54 years of age because of the injury to his neck and spine sustained when his horse Sein threw him. When they returned to the farm, the rest of the summer was spent helping the children recover from the whooping cough. Other entries for that summer stated that George went to Flora to sing with the Bunch Grass Quartet, that the family attended the Chatauqua in Joseph and that he and Nellie cleaned the schoolhouse for the fall term. One summer Sunday the Seventh Day Adventists baptized new members in Deer Creek. Everyone attended even though no one in the family was a member of that sect; and all enjoyed the picnic that followed. The annual visit of the Watkins Man (a rural peddler of sundries, liniments, medicines and flavorings) was recorded. Also George noted that he cut loads of small pine trees to be used for road building.

Then in 1918 came the great flu epidemic, and the family moved to town where there was a hospital in Enterprise which helped care for George during his siege with flu and pneumonia. In the early part of 1919, George and Nellie went to California with the idea of relocating in Long Beach. Many family members lived in Los Angeles, and some had benefited by the Signal Hill oil discovery. Time was not right for such a move, although George's health was periled by the winter climate in Eastern Oregon.

The final change, though, was the increasingly heavy routine of the farm. Following the flu epidemic, they did return to the farm and take up the routine of living in Enterprise during the school year and in Paradise in late spring, summer, and early fall. Food supplies were prepared for the months spent in town. Chickens were canned, fruit and vegetables were canned, jellies and jams were made, meat was processed, eggs were preserved, corn and apples were dried and flour milled. The store of apples and potatoes was periodically replenished in the town house. Early fall was a busy time hauling to market the produce of the farm. Load after load of wheat was taken to the Oregon Short Line Railroad in Enterprise. Sometimes the hogs were driven on foot and sometimes hauled by wagon, a distance of fifty miles through the forest reserve. Cattle were driven on the hoof to market. Much produce, such as apples and potatoes, butter and eggs and animal feed was sold locally.

The calendars reflect the many trivial items that made up the daily routine of working the land as well as the important changes that had come over the family itself. *Finally, the time arrived when*

*the accumulation of moves to accommodate school demands, over-
come sickness, and avoid heavy routine meant that the family would
leave the farm forever.*

(Mary Belle Fielding)

The point is a relatively simple one, and the author has built her
case with supporting examples which she gleaned from family calendars.
By the time we finish the exposition, we understand what she meant
when in the opening paragraph she stated in the thesis that the family
had gradually, not suddenly, decided to leave the farm. By breaking the
idea of arriving gradually at a decision into the various steps--firstly, the
growing need of the children to attend school; secondly, George's
gradually declining health; and thirdly, George's declining ability to deal
with the heavy routine of the farm--each of which she clearly announces
at the beginning of each support paragraph, the author has broken down
the main idea into sub-ideas that she supports. Actually, while the
writer has used process to make her basic point, she could as easily have
presented this as a causal paper or a paper that would show in this case
a relationship between several causes and one effect. The thesis would
have been a statement somewhat to the effect that there were three factors that led George and his family to leave the farm: the first was the
children's need for education, the second was George's declining health,
and the third was the increasingly heavy demands of running the farm.
Or the author could have broken the various increasing demands on
George into three kinds: health, familial, and farm. This would have
resulted in a classification paper. Certain subjects lend themselves
naturally to certain kinds of papers. But in many cases, it is really a matter of choice.   There are, though, some basic rules to remember about
each of these various types.

Example: Make certain that each example directly relates to the
point being made and that all the examples are filled with details that
bring to life the historical past. Only through careful research can you
really know what people did, wore, felt, and experienced in the past.
The details must be vivid and true to the historical past.

Process: Think through the subject carefully so that you know that
you have all the steps in mind. Then state those steps clearly and with a
sense of order. In the case of those steps that led to George's leaving the
farm, the chronological method of ordering would be the easiest although we could present them in an increasing order of severity, leading
from the easiest for George to deal with to the most difficult. Think of
yourself as giving instructions to someone who does not understand or
know the process. What may be very clear to you may not be clear to the
reader.

Classification: If you are going to classify, remember that you must
deal with the total subject and you must classify on the basis of one principle. To present in the same paper the demands on George along with
the demands on the farm hands would be to introduce a second prin-

ciple of classification. We are interested only in those demands placed on George, and we are interested in all of them.

Causal Analysis: Avoid being simplistic. Remember that life is complex, and writing about people and their motives from the distance of time is fraught with dangers. George may have left the farm for all of the reasons we have discussed, but then he may have simply left because he was bored with farm life and wanted a change. And most of all, avoid reading our own ideologies and prejudices into the lives of our ancestors.

Comparison and/or contrast: Compare or contrast two subjects on the basis of the same criterion. To contrast George's failing health with his brother's financial success is to say little or nothing. Compare or contrast George's ability to deal with the challenges of his farm with his brother's ability to deal with his own challenges in running a farm; that way the discussion has point and purpose.

The beginning writer has only to consider a few pages of one of the several good family expositions available to discover that most professional writers employ all of these forms of exposition, sometimes even mixing various forms in one section. MacFarlane in his *The Family Life of Ralph Josselin* begins one paragraph with the statement "Contacts with neighbors were of many kinds." Then he proceeds in a classical classification paragraph to give examples of each specific kind: they borrowed things, they helped with chores, they made loans, they provided medical help, and they gave emotional support. Each of these sub-ideas is followed by specific details. He compares Josselin to other clergy and yeomen: "We may now compare Josselin's economic position with that of other clergy and yeomen, and with the other inhabitants of Earls Colne." He discusses his tax assessments and his nonfarming income, driving home the basic comparison/contrast of how Josselin's economic position differed from or was similar to other clergy and yeomen. He employs causal analysis: "One of the chief causes for his constant state of watchfulness and worry, was that the world of phenomena was seen as purposeful and comprehensible," then turns to the effects that this cause brought about. And throughout the book, he uses examples to back up the basic abstract points he makes. Good expository writing is a mixture of many types.

The analysis of genealogical records is an exciting but demanding task. It requires imagination and a willingness to test the limits of the documents, even to the point at which many would strongly disagree with the character development or the plot. And the writer prepares himself through careful research as well as by developing his analytical abilities. Another important ingredient is careful preparation in background materials on the period and area on which he is writing (See Chapter 4: "Point of View"). Above all, the writer must push the documents as far as he can in order to discover patterns that relate to the family or to the individual: the Alsatian couple that takes fifty years to make the transition from France to America; the quiet, simple German-speaking farmer who spends his entire life in a small German-speaking community, dying in the womb of mother church, never far from his native land and native culture; the well-dressed, perhaps vain Maine colonial who dies almost insolvent at the time of the Revolution, leaving his daughter married to a young revolutionary soldier who eventually goes to Canada only to be executed for raping a woman. Then and only then is the writer in a position to develop a character and to construct a plot. We may feel that both character and plot are out of line with historical fact or so conjectural that we protest that the record has been violated. Certainly, we want the character developed or the plot itself to be in line with what we know historically. Williams's portrait of Elisha Partridge, for example, is simply not justified by the record, but as a novelist his portrait is legitimate. Above all, we must remember that we are learning how to tell a story, and some may elect to tell a story that is technically not true while others may feel that they can proceed no farther than the record allows. And there will be those who will work within these extremes, those who never violate the spirit of the historical record but who in detail, character, and plot fill in the historical gaps.

Once the writer has arrived at this point, he has also begun to develop a character, to see a historical personality in time and space. This marriage of character and plot is the point at which one begins to build a story, the point at which the facts and the dates begin to give rise to a narrative. We now have a window into the psyche of the family. We understand. We analyze. And the portrait of a personality begins to form in our minds.

BIBLIOGRAPHY: GENERAL ANALYTICAL WORKS

Ladurie, Emmanuel Le Roy. *Montaillou, The Promised Land of Error.* Translated by Barbara Bray. New York: Vintage Books, 1979.
A fascinating study of a small French village of some 600 years ago. Relying on accounts now in Vatican repositories, the author gives us a vivid picture of the day-by-day life of very ordinary and common people.

Laslett, Peter. *The World We Have Lost.* London: Methuen and Company Limited, 1971.
A fascinating if somewhat romantic analysis of pre-Industrial Revolution England with some comparisons with twentieth-century English society.

CHAPTER 3

WRITING THE NARRATIVE

We have discussed genealogical and local history sources and social, familial, and personality patterns that emerge from the data, and I have suggested several specific ones: the relationship between the origin of the family and its pattern of settlement, how the family earned and spent money, what the family considered important or valuable, and what kind of social and personality traits the family exhibited. There are, obviously, other possibilities, probably as varied and numerous as the families and personalities that we are writing about. For example, it is fashionable to speak of a man's "mid-life crisis" or of the family's first-born being "fortune's favorite." Feminists complain of masculine bias, and some men persist despite all kinds of evidence to the contrary in analyzing feminine behavior in terms of "that time of the month." We describe friends or relatives as "born with a silver spoon in their mouths," as "losers," or simply as "unlucky in life." On a literary and more sophisticated level, critics see Hamlet, King Lear, Macbeth, and Othello as possessed of a tragic flaw. Whether sophisticated or not, the approach is really the same, namely to bring the mass of information about a person's life or a family into some kind of comprehensible focus.

As we experience life, we mentally distinguish between those events and personalities that are insignificant trivia and those that have become important and memorable to us. In other words, we constantly bring our own private experiences into focus by seeing events and people in certain patterns. The points of focus are hardly ever intellectual or scientific. Rather, we conceptualize things or persons as frightening or pleasant, dangerous and hostile, or warm and comfortable. The fact is that we are constantly engaged in a myriad of tasks that we probably could not remember even if we tried, and the only way that we can reasonably deal with our environment is to package or categorize its events. We rise at a certain time in the morning, eat breakfast, and commute to work; we spend eight hours meeting the demands of an employer, punch out, and drive home. We would hardly call all of these events worthy of record in and of themselves. Most we forget, but some do get recorded in our memories in categories of pleasantness, comfort, danger, excitation, or disgust. One school of psychotherapy--Ellis's Rational Emotive Therapy--argues that events or external stimuli have no significance in and of themselves except as we interpret them or give them value or significance. Thus a situation or person is not necessarily hostile or inviting except as we interpret or see it as hostile or inviting. Basically the writer takes much the same approach in constructing a narrative: either he begins by focusing on certain "important" events and thus sees a segment in time in terms of a plot or by focusing initially on certain individual qualities and thus gives rise to a characterization.

One way of focusing on life's events is to evaluate them in terms of emotional intensity. The birth of a child, a marriage, a career preparation, a divorce, or a death are all in themselves emotionally charged events. Further, these events are not isolated but are instead preceded and followed by events that lead into and follow from such moments of emotional intensity. Marriage results from a series of events: one early becomes aware of sexual feelings and begins to talk to members of the opposite sex, eventually dating. Dating leads to a more serious consideration, several broken and successful relationships, the acceptance or rejection by the families involved, and ultimately to marriage itself.

Russell Baker's *Growing Up* is an example of focusing the events of one's life and writing about themes that have some emotional intensity. Largely an autobiography (although there are biographical elements in Baker's descriptions of his mother), *Growing Up* is the story of Baker's early years leading up to his marriage. There are many incidents that he could relate about his younger years, but the focus that naturally dominates the book is the story of his sexual maturation. Baker's description of one of his friend's successes with women and of his Uncle Jack's attempts to tell him about the "facts of life" come midway through the book, but these events lead to a later brush with a sordid, well-dressed stranger and then on to more legitimate sexual encounters when Baker is serving in the naval air force, and these encounters precede his meeting of Mimi. Mimi provides, in some sense, the pivotal center and logical conclusion of the book as Baker describes her disastrous first meeting with his mother, the other dominant female force in his autobiography. Mimi lives with another girl in an apartment downtown, and in Mrs. Baker's view she uses too much makeup, she deters Russell from making something of himself, and under Mimi's influence Russell acts too much like his deceased father. In the final chapter, Baker draws the theme of his sexual maturation together with all the other themes of the book. In telling his own life story, there were countless trivial experiences that Baker could well have mentioned but which he does not because they do not bear on the focus of sexual maturation.

When the writer draws a life portrait, a characterization, he quickly recognizes that each individual's personality is dominated by certain qualities or traits. Let us assume that two people through years of emotional stress and indecision have married. That marriage, because of the career demands of the husband and the conflicting intellectual and cultural tastes of the wife, is followed with years of poor adjustment and misunderstanding. Children come into the family, and the husband pursues his personal dream across different countries and through several states recognizing, but unable to satisfy, the needs of his wife; all the time the misunderstanding grows until the maladjustment reaches a climax or a point from which neither can retreat and follows both husband and wife down to death. Certainly this focusing on several but limited traits may be artificial or at least highly biased, but the reader needs this kind of direction if he is to understand someone in the limited space of a story.

Wallace Stegner's *Angle of Repose* is a narrative built around two characterizations; the story, which shows the gradual decline of the relationship, is a series of succeeding points of misunderstanding leading to the inevitable climax or conclusion. Stegner really makes only one point: that two people of such different backgrounds and dispositions will eventually work toward a life of permanent misunderstanding:

> "So they lived happily-unhappily ever after," I said. "Year after irrelevant year, half a century almost, through one world war and through the Jazz Age and through the Depression and the New Deal and all that; through Prohibition and Women's Rights, through the automobile and the radio and television and into the second world war. Through all those changes, and not a change in them."
>
> (Wallace Stegner, *Angle of Repose*)

Stegner, by selecting and arranging the episodes or scenes in his novel, shows that these lives were shattered by their widely divergent and contrasting backgrounds and interests.

The fact is that we relate better to people than we do to action. And a sensitive rendering of a personality set in significant action--events of emotional intensity--strikes us as having more depth than a story that focuses on action for the sake of action alone. When it comes to the family narrative, most people have lived somewhat action-limited lives. There is normally not much that we can find that sets our ancestors' lives off as adventurous. But there is always the interest that we can naturally have in understanding someone who lived in the past. An example of this technique of awakening our interest by focusing on specific character qualities is C. David Heymann's series of biographies in his *American Aristocracy: The Lives and Times of James Russell, Amy, and Robert Lowell* (New York: Dodd, Mead & Co., 1980).

The reader has only to open to the table of contents to see how the author builds each biography around a single personality trait or characteristic: "James Russell Lowell, The Natural Aristocrat," "Amy Lowell, Last of the Barons," and "Robert Lowell, Noble Savage." The short biographies that precede the three major biographies of the book are also built around single points of focus. Percival Lowle is seen primarily as a settler, John Lowell as a reverend, and his son John Lowell as a judge. Each of these individuals played several conflicting and simultaneously compatible roles, but the author has chosen for the sake of clarity to see each from a single character focus.

Most writers when they begin a story conceptualize first a personality. Once they have a firm grasp of the character, the action proceeds almost naturally. Still, advancing the story is such a natural blending of character and plot that to separate one from the other or to maintain that one approach is better or naturally first is to deny the delicate balance that occurs when a writer develops a story. He may begin with a character or characters, but it is almost impossible to see that character except in action and plot.

CHARACTERIZATION

When it comes to characterization or the focusing of a character, there are three basic matters to consider. The first, maintaining the delicate balance between consistency and complexity, is important when presenting a character either in exposition or narrative. The second, dealing with the scarcity of available material, is particularly true of family history. And the third, whether to use dialogue and thought, action, description, or direct exposition to present a character, is true of both fiction and family history.

Consistency Versus Complexity. The writer of the family narrative—if he expects to develop a character that is both historically accurate and believable—must draw a portrait that is a blend of good and bad qualities as well as consistent in personality. We expect a Revolutionary War soldier to be, after all, consistently a soldier, and we expect a mother to exhibit the normal qualities of motherhood, but no human being has ever been totally good or totally bad no matter how famous or infamous. The beginning writer, particularly when he is dealing with members of his own family, often cannot resist the temptation to present family members in stereotypical strokes. Typically he might draw his mother as an angel of mercy and his stepfather as a villain of repression although in reality both parents fed into and maintained one another's personalities. Moreover, while real individuals alternate between admirable and socially unacceptable qualities (complexity), they are normally a fairly predictable blend of those qualities (consistency). People exhibit personality traits that follow them throughout life although they do undergo gradual but perceptible changes. Unfortunate personal choices may drive the once compulsive bread-winner to abandon his family, but they do not totally alter that man's basic personality. The popularly construed "mid-life crisis" impacts all men differently according to the peculiar mix of each man's personality. How, however, does one provide a smooth mixing of consistency and complexity in characterizing a historical personality?

For many years, my family guarded a secret about one Joseph Farrow, a native of Massachusetts and Maine who settled on Prince Edward Island somewhere around 1791. Most knew in the family that Joseph Farrow had died of "unfortunate circumstances" and that his widowed wife, Judith Partridge Farrow, had thereafter married my paternal ancestor John Gouldrup. The intriguing question was what were the "unfortunate circumstances"; those who knew simply refused to share the information. Some suggested in hushed tones that Joseph Farrow had raped a woman and had been hanged for the crime, but the actual circumstances were never really clear. Not much was known about this Joseph Farrow except that he probably served in 1795 in Bridge's Regiment of Foot for Massachusetts, that he lived with his wife in 1790 near Pemaquid Pond in Waldoboro, Lincoln County, Maine, and that his wife, after his death on Prince Edward Island, had their three children baptized into St. Paul's Anglican Church. It seemed to be generally concluded that this roughened Revolutionary War veteran who neglected his wife's sensitivities by refusing to have his children baptized properly had committed the heinous crime of rape shortly after arriving on Prince Edward Island (character consistency). With time and the refusal of some family members to search further into the circumstances of the alleged rape, Joseph Farrow took on all the stereotypical qualities of a perverted rapist. A second possibility, just as much a stereotypical portrait, also suggested itself. Perhaps Joseph, a patriotic American and veteran of the Colonial Army, had been framed. After all, Prince Edward Island had remained loyal to the crown, a haven for many loyalist families.

To present a historical figure as a perverted criminal or as an innocent victim of a mob was simply too pat, too consistent. Luckily, a record of the trial as well as a newspaper account of the entire affair including the hanging has survived, and the characterization that emerges from its pages is not so simple; indeed, it introduces the very valuable element of complexity. A trial was held, and the court ruled that Joseph Farrow was guilty of rape, condemning him to die by hanging on Monday, July 30, 1792, for being so "moved and seduced by the instigation of the devil" that he "with force and arms ... did ravish and carnally know" one Elizabeth Beers. The newspaper account adds even more damning facts: Elizabeth Beers was only twelve years old, and she had the reputation of being "perfectly innocent and decent," a young girl on whom "not even the foul breath of fame had ever dared to blow"; a young boy of seventeen had witnessed the entire sordid affair; and Joseph Farrow had had literally nothing to say in vindication of himself during the trial and had shortly after the trial dashed any possible sympathy for himself by shamelessly attempting to escape. As far as the framed-patriotic-American theory goes, the victim's surname, Beers, would suggest such a possibility. There were two loyalist Beers families on Prince Edward Island, and one of the two heads of families, a certain Ensign Joseph Beers, did serve as high sheriff of Queens County. The problem with this interpretation is that there is nothing in the record to indicate that Joseph Beers was sheriff at the time of Joseph's trial nor that he had a daughter named Elizabeth.

The newspaper account (*Royal Gazette, and Miscellany of the Island of Saint John*, July 30, 1792) adds some tantalizing details that move the characterization forever from the stereotypical or the realm of consistency to that of a blend of consistency and complexity. First, there was enough public sympathy for Joseph Farrow to cause some men to circulate a petition "in his behalf" although Farrow's attempt to escape dashed all hopes of any pardon. And a few moments before Joseph Farrow was led to the gallows, a minister paid him a last visit, and as the minister left him, Joseph put a paper into his hands, the substance of which follows:

> That notwithstanding he was condemned to die for a rape, he declared to the world he was not guilty of this crime. He hoped that it might be a warning to all beholders, and the means of awakening them to those important duties which the Spirit of our holy Religion requires, and which could be attained only through the merits of a blessed Redeemer. It had pleased God to awake him to a sense of his unworthiness by a heavy stroke; but he desired to praise His holy Name for His loving kindness, and for all His mercies manifested towards him. He observed, that it would hereafter be said, that Farrow was hung--but it was better, he said for him to die now, with an interest in the blessed Jesus, than to have a longer continuance in sin. I desire, says he, gratefully to praise God for having graciously brought me to a sight of my lost state by nature, and enabled me to lay hold on the Rock of my Salvation.

And then, Joseph after addressing himself to Judith his wife whom the article describes as "wretchedly distressed," continued the letter:

> My dear wife, I pray that you would not mourn for me--but mourn rather for yourself. Be earnest in prayer to God, that he would, for his dear Son's sake, who was crucified for the Redemption of the world, make us all partakers of his heavenly glory. I pray that you would not give "Sleep to your Eyes, nor Slumber to your Eyelids, till you find Peace to your Soul"--I pray that you and all others may take this to heart, and search and try yourselves. This from your dying husband Joseph Farrow.

It is difficult, the article continues, to reconcile this letter with Joseph's behavior during the trial. Not once did he even endeavor to vindicate himself.

Difficult is not the word. Perhaps impossible. Certainly impossible from the vantage point of two hundred years. But this incident has all the makings of a superb characterization. It would have been easy to stereotype Joseph Farrow as an unfeeling, perverted brute or even as a veteran of the American colonial army trapped by the hostile environment of loyalist Prince Edward Island. Why did Joseph Farrow not speak out in his defense during the trail? And why were there no witnesses in his behalf? Had he committed some kind of indiscretion? But what about the petition "in his behalf"? What about the testimony of the witnesses? What about Farrow's "wretchedly distressed" wife and his "three little, helpless, innocent babes"? What about Farrow's religious sentiments: were they cliches and formulae or the sentiments of a deeply religious person? Was this a man caught in a vortex that was beyond his capacity to comprehend? Even the newspaper in its final comments leaves the impression that the truth is not easy to arrive at in this case:

> It is difficult to reconcile the last words of this dying man, with his behavior on the trial, where he did not even endeavor to vindicate himself. It would be unnecessary to comment on this circumstance--we leave it to every one to weigh as they think most proper--and shall only observe, that as it is not the lot of mortality to be omniscient, so it is our duty neither to attack the innocent, or defend the guilty.

Whatever the final portrait, the character that emerges from the facts and details of this account must be complex indeed, a far cry from the perverted rapist or framed American who so many people chose to conjure up. The ideal characterization, then, is a portrait that reaches beyond the stereotypical to blend and balance consistency with complexity and sets that character in significant action or into events of high emotional intensity: Joseph was probably guilty of some indiscretion, yet he was neither the simple, stereotypical villain nor framed innocent. But complexity must never be sacrificed to the fantastical: whatever he did wrong, it remained safely within the limits of normal human indiscretion. And whatever he was, even if he did rape a twelve-year-old girl, he was still the father of "innocent" children, the husband of a loving wife, a deeply religious person, and good enough to awaken popular sympathy among the people of Charlottetown, Prince Edward Island.

Still, there are cases in which the writer's perception of a person is either largely positive or largely negative, and to presume that the writer must see something else is to destroy what is essential about the reality of the author's powers of perception and about the way in which it relates or related to that other person. In other words, the characterization, particularly in the family narrative, is as much a judgment of the writer as it is of the person being characterized; and it is just possible that for many writers one cannot expect much more than the absolutely negative or positive portrait. Yet even here the author must rise above the stereotypical if the characterizations are to succeed. The following prose-poetic descriptions preceded by a prose preface describing the family illustrate how the consistently negative or positive portrait can rise above the stereotypical. The student combines a prose prologue with three poems on her mother, seven poems about her siblings, and one last poem about her father, which taken all together seem to give a balanced description of a family, yet "Ghetto Family" is primarily a portrait of the mother. Because our interest is in the characterizations of the mother and the father, I have omitted the seven poems about the author's siblings.

Ghetto Family

Preface

We had moved up from the lower east side to a lower Harlem flat with the luxury of a toilet and bath. The discomfort of the move on a cold blustery New York day was matched by the argument between my father speaking in a broken English dialect and Mrs. Clavins shouting in a brogue. She flailed out at us reiterating, "I count five children, not three." Despite Mrs. Clavins, we were to become a family of eight children in the next six years. To some people it was a Jewish ghetto, to others an Irish, Italian slum. It was home to us.

The move was also notable for the illnesses that followed in its wake. Baby brother Lou, not yet three, had been ailing and was hospitalized with diphtheria within three days. I followed by two days with a mismatched case of scarlet fever. We were removed to a cluster of hospitals on Randalls Island for the treatment of contagious diseases. Our flat and dwelling were posted with quarantine notices.

When we had finally settled in and taken stock of our surroundings, we noted the fire and police stations across the street. School was within walking distance.

The police station afforded a daily view of the sorry scheme of things: disorderly drunks, errant youths, lost children, and once a lifeless boy recovered from the East River. This scene stayed with me as I had become aware of death in the desiccated bodies of stray cats and dogs left on the street, a horse fallen in the gutter.

The fire station offered a contrast with its clanging alarm bell, the high spirited horses, charging out, the steamer belching fire and sparks.

Mama was the center of our universe. She put all her energies into our upbringing. It was possible to endure poverty, its rats, roaches, bedbugs, even the explosive outbursts of papa. These could be suffered as long as she was there.

Mama was a quiet person. Indeed, there was not time for chats, no time for play with the children. We older ones took up the slack in looking after them. I remember mama always pregnant, her red hands in the washtubs, or nursing the baby at her breast, soothing the frightened toddler who had ventured out too far. Most of all, she kept us out of papa's way. Without verbalizing, mama let us feel that she was our ally in the never ending threat of papa's runaway temper. She rarely laughed, but so delightfully distinctive was her laughter that it still echoes in my mind.

Childhood was a compendium of school days, some truly inspiring, some to be endured, some a refuge from reality and fears. The days were brightened by the noon hours. Mama said she knew when I was home because I invariably sent out in advance, "I'm hungry." Lunch hour was safe, mama was there, papa was not.

Childhood was a calendar of humdrum days slashed by the lightning of papa's fury, the terrible trauma of mama's illness and her loss. Those six years are deeply etched in my memory and in my psyche.

Tenement Mother

Hands chafed by ribbed washboard
she labored late over iron tub
until back and legs gave.
Nights she walked rough wooden floors
tending her brood. Sweet tea
for small complaints, cool hands
for fevered head.
Her heart wore down bearing children
two years apart; one held in arms,
a second tugging at her skirt,
the third kicking in her womb.
Cautioned she would not survive
another birth, her husband said
nature will not be denied.
In her fortieth year she bore
her eighth. Heart broken, died.

Mama

I rocked
in your cradle nine months,
drinking your essence,
drawing your strength.
Cradled in your arms,
you shone down
enveloping me.
Again your body
hummed with life,

your arms enclosing another.
Eight times
you carried us through
the nurturing waters,
eight times, mother.
You were there
yesterday and before;
at your side
there was always tomorrow.
When the wild wind
blew out your light,
our house went dark,
mama, mama.

The Dress

When did mama find time,
she with her roughened hands
deep in the iron tub,
scrubbing the ghetto grime
to a chastened white,
running the endless laundry line
across the concrete yard,
carrying coal from basement bin
to the fifth floor flat,
always with child
and the toddler at her back?
When did she find time
to ride the clattering treadle,
to shape and sew the perfect dress,
a creamy poplin, piped in red,
a dress for a ragged child
to dream on, a dream
for her waking up,
when did mama find time?

In the prose prologue and the three initial poems, the author's perception of her mother is clearly positive. The seven poems about the author's brothers and sisters appear at this point. We have had some clear indications of the character of the father, but the description of the father reveals now the reasons for the almost uniformly negative perception of the writer:

To My Father

I knew you
in the only way I could;

the sound of your voice
tearing down the quiet,
leaving me helpless
before the lightning
of your rage.
You unmade
the fragile years
of my childhood,
dimmed the infrequent
brightness of my days.
I grew lopsided,
fearing the blow,
the prurient touch,
the warp of hate.
The silence came at last,
You could not outshout death.
You left me nothing to remember,
too much to forget.

(Edith Mendez)

In describing her parents, the author presents her father as consistently and painfully negative and her mother as consistently positive. Yet the characterizations are not of an oversimplified villain and angel largely because when combined with the prose preface, they describe a pathetically oppressed mother whose passivity allows the totalitarian and abusive exploitation of the family by the father. Few would venture to record the kinds of feelings that this student has recorded, and while her father certainly must have possessed some redeeming qualities, the total impact that the father had on the author was apparently consistently negative. Perhaps a biographer writing from a more neutral distance would find some positive personality qualities in the father, but to ask the victim of such an experience to do much more than she has done would be to ask her to violate the veracity of her own personal powers of perception. After all, her father did abuse her.

What gives these prose and poetic accounts, then, the feel of truth is not only the sense of stark realism: it is more that they are a totally accurate description of an abusive triangle. Her descriptions, while certainly very negative in the case of the father, are intricately detailed and as a result very realistic. The essence of blending consistency with complexity then is to arrive at a detailed description, in this case a description of a woman struggling to give direction to the children she is consistently forced to bring into the world and whom she cannot adequately protect from their father.

Contrast this characterization of the mother with the following account. Here the student depicts a daughter and mother in stereotypical and abstract strokes that lead the reader to wonder if the characters depicted really ever lived:

Elisa May Manwaring was a woman with strong courage, great determination and complete faith in God and His goodness. All of these virtues were wrapped with a happy disposition and a very ready laugh. She had many friends who loved her dearly. Her family would have done almost anything to make her happy, but she was so independent that she seldom asked for help. Rather, she turned to help others in her most trying hours.

Elisa May had been raised by a widowed mother, Augusta Elizabeth Manwaring, whose life was full of turmoil and heavy labor. She had a strong belief in God, and knew that somehow, with His divine love for all His children, He would help her.

This woman and her mother are simply too good to be real. No one would deny that these descriptions contain elements of truth, but the characters who emerge are boringly and consistently good. Elisa May would never commit a sin. She would never lose faith under trying circumstances. There was never anything but love and happiness in her relationships. And she was ruggedly self-reliant. There is absolutely nothing negative or complex or even human about either of the two women. In this characterization, if we could call it such, consistency is pushed to its ultimate.

The flaw in this characterization, though, is not simply that the author has seen these two women as uniformly positive. The author of the prose-poetic "Ghetto Family" is certainly uniformly positive in describing the mother. The basic weakness is that the two characterizations of Elisa May and Augusta Elizabeth Manwaring never leave the abstract or generalized level, thus resulting in characterizations that are consistently stereotypical. The author sees and describes both only in terms that are on the highest level of abstraction: "strong courage," "great determination," "complete faith," "happy disposition," "ready laugh," "independent," "life . . . full of turmoil and heavy labor," and "strong belief in God." We really wonder if the writer ever knew these two women. Contrast these generalizations with the author's use of significant detail or detail with emotional intensity in the "Ghetto Family": "ribbed washboard," "the third kicking in her womb," "nature will not be denied," "roughened hands deep in the iron tub," "the clattering treadle," "your voice tearing down the quiet," and "the prurient touch." Essentially, the difference is detail, and detail results in family history only when the writer gives himself up completely to his subject matter. Through research or careful analysis, he becomes such a part of the historical past that he cannot escape the myriad of details that flood his mind. What gives writing power is detail. We might even buy some of these stereotypical consistencies if we could just once see these people described in detail. As it is, we rebel in anger and frustration, and we doubt if these stereotypical people ever did live.

Dealing with Limited Source Materials: the Static or Dynamic Characterization. By definition, a static characterization presents a personality that does not change while a dynamic characterization involves some kind of basic personality change. While either depends to some extent on the skill of the writer, each is more directly dependent on the length of the story: a short story, because of the lack of space, shows little if any change in a character; a story of greater length such as a novel has sufficient space in which to show a significant and definite personality change. In family narration, there is a more limiting problem: once the writer moves much beyond his immediate family members, people with whom he has had personal or extensive contact, he finds it difficult to gather enough material to develop a dynamic character. The author of the "Ghetto Family" could easily have developed dynamic characterizations in most of her subjects, but she elected to show each character in static portraits. In the case of Joseph Farrow, however, we have only one brief glimpse (and this is afforded by the happy circumstances of a published note in a contemporary newspaper) into the character of a man. It would take several letters and notes to allow us to see a gradual change in this subject. Obviously, a dynamic characterization is the happier choice, but no one would argue that a brief glimpse into the life of a man who lived two centuries ago is indeed wonderful and is material for a truly excellent story. In family narration, the choice of whether to develop a dynamic character or a static character is decided largely by the amount of source material available.

Simply put, the writer must have sufficient material at his disposal if he is to show any kind of change in a character, and the information must be personal and detailed enough to allow the writer to establish the exact nature of the change. One of the best sources of this kind of information is the letter, and typical of this kind of source are the letters of Thomas Wells written to members of his family during the years 1862 through 1864 while he served with a northern unit in the Civil War. His personal and detailed letters are priceless documents that show the life of a common soldier as well as the kinds of character development a person of over a century ago underwent. Specifically, Thomas Wells encountered challenges and difficulties that altered him as a person. They did not change his basic personality, but they did change him.

The Civil War was for Thomas Wells a great personal challenge, but it was not the combat, the death, and the senseless destruction of property that impacted him. Judging from his letters, his tenure in the military was generally one of inclement weather, long marches, terrible food, and diarrhea. Of greater impact was the death of his mother, his gnawing homesickness, the marriage of a young lady with whom he had been romantically involved, and his constant struggle with ill health. Perhaps the best way to show the subtle but perceptible change in Thomas Wells is to quote from some of his letters.

After a brief salutation, his letter of 11 February 1862 complains of lameness and a sore throat. "I took some olive tar for it," he writes, "and it made me sick to my stomjack. I was so sick that I could not eat any breakfast this morning but I feal better now this is all that I can think of now giv my lov all yours." His letters throughout 1862 are not much longer although by November he is going into much more detail about the military experience. Still the themes remain pretty much the same-- complaints of health problems and the lack of letters from home:

> I am well at present, but hav not been very well for the past weak. I hav been on duty all the time, but it was very hard for me for I could hardly stand up some of the time but I was determined to stick it through if I could. I went to the doctors and got some medicin, but it did me no good, so I took a does of pills that I brought from home and . . . I hav felt firstrate since yesterday noon. . . . . I hav not recived a singal letter from iny one for more then 2 weaks, untill I recived yours last night. I was begining to think that I was forgotton intirly.
>
> (Letter of 16 December 1862)

With the new year, his letters still sound on the same themes, but new elements begin to be a part of his correspondence. Now he writes of minor skirmishes with the enemy--there is really never a full-scale battle. He complains about the endless war and threatens to take a "french furlow" and "leave for they are not going to stay and fight for theas fig Officers . . ." (Letter of 10 January 1863). While it is hard to judge, he battles what appears to be a series of migraine headaches. With time his letters exhibit a gradual shift from an emphasis on his physical needs and problems to the war about him. In his letter of 23 March 1863, he sketches out a map of the camp, and in April, he helps give chase to a party of rebels (Letter of 19 April 1863). His letters now are longer and more detailed although they still speak of occasional bouts with ill heath, the lack of food, and his need for a constant flow of letters from home. On 2 June 1863 he enters the hospital for a long stay. He is vague about the actual illness, but it appears to be more of his same general intestinal problems. His weight drops to 150 pounds, and he has a constant struggle trying to build up his strength (Letter of 14 June 1863). Though all his letters, we begin to detect two basic personality traits, both of which with time become more pronounced.

Thomas loves to listen to preachers and he loves to give preachy advice even when it makes him appear a bit hypocritical. He has no problem complaining about his sister's spelling although his is a bit unorthodox. And he does not want his sister to leave home to work in Chicago even when he is trooping all over the South undoubtedly driving his parents to distraction with his letters of life-threatening illnesses. Sitting now in the comfort of a hospital with excellent food, light guard duty, and a daily pass to town, he waxes eloquent attacking those who would seek a reasonable peace over a total military victory:

I should like to see some of them down here, caring a gun, and a 50 pound knapsack a while, for I think they are neaded down here in Uncle Sams servis, and are no better I think to fight for their Country then we are but they are backbighting, smooth tonged, cowardly, pimp, and dosent show their heads down here in dixey.

(Letter of 14 June 1863)

When his sister Mary becomes involved with a Mr. Hastings, Thomas advises her to beware of "wild chaps" and "to set a good example to our Dear Sister Elvira and little brothers . . ." (Letter of 24 January 1864). His sister had apparently, at this point, had enough because she then in turn suggests that he had been too intimate with his cousin, evoking a long self-righteous and defensive sermon (Letter of 19 April 1864). His trait of sermonizing grows only more pronounced as time wears on, a trait brought on no doubt by his growing sense of manhood and his feeling that now, with the death of his mother and the brooding sense of loss his father was experiencing, he was the head of the family.

Thomas has another trait that becomes more pronounced with the many problems and challenges he encounters. In 1862, he is a young, frightened boy thinking only of his own physical needs. But he very quickly becomes a mature adult moving from a constantly sick boy to a healthy, independent man. He sincerely and genuinely provides mature comfort to his father on the loss of his mother (Letter of 11 October 1863). But the clearest signal of his growing maturity and independence is his letter of 24 January 1864 in which he tells his family that he will not be able to come home until April or May because of the difficulty of travel; only a few short months before he was so homesick and disgusted with the war that he was considering taking a "french furlow." He now accepts the news that his former girlfriend is married with absolute self-control: "it did not trouble me in the least" (Letter of 6 April 1864); as far as he is concerned, there is plenty of time to marry. The two years of military service moved him from a young, frightened homesick boy with migraine headaches and a constant intestinal disorder to a healthy, independent adult who can take the death of his mother and the loss of a girlfriend in stride.

Thomas Wells's basic personality did not change in the two years: he continued to be concerned with matters of health and letters from home. But the war turned him into an independent and self-reliant man, although it also strengthened his trait of giving advice even when it was neither wanted nor appreciated. His letters reveal a dynamic and changing personality.

Another excellent source of information, sufficient enough to allow a writer to show a character in change, is the journal. Often, however, an individual leaves years unrecorded, and when he finally is able to take the time to fill in the missing years, the resulting record is the product of one character perspective, and it becomes impossible to see that character in change. One good example of this is William Grant (1838-1916) who did not begin his journal until he was forty-four years old. Although he then continued to maintain it for almost thirty years until the age of seventy-two, six years before he died, the character perspective is the same for the first forty-four years of his life. He commenced his journal with a sense of optimism that is typical of men at the height of their personal powers, and almost everything he remembered about the period before he began his journal reflected this sense of optimism.

According to his own summary of his life at the age of forty-four, he was born in England on Christmas day to the sound of church bells and carols. "All years were full of bright hope . . . as I believed in a future greatness." By the time he turned seven, he had begun to show strong talent for music and to display a native intelligence in the local "Sabbath school." Despite his small size and lack of formal education, he recounted how, in 1847, his "master's family" told him that he would make a "splendid Methodist parson." When he wrote in detail of the horror of cholera and the literally scores of friends and relatives who died all about him, he credited his survival to his personal faith. He did become ill but recovered almost immediately, telling his family that if they had had faith like his, all would have recovered.

It was in 1850 when he was thirteen that he first came into contact with Mormonism. He listened and began to assimilate its principles causing a bit of a doctrinal stir as he had by now "gained the highest class" in the Methodist Sabbath school being, in his words, "one of the best scholars in the 2nd class of Bibles." When he was fourteen, he attended the first World's International Exhibition at Hyde Park, drinking in the excitement of new ideas. He began a small personal library and even began to take an active interest in politics. At fifteen he changed his trade from that of curry-comb making to padlock making. He became a Mormon Sunday school teacher, learned music notation, and did some itinerant preaching. By 1853, when he was sixteen, he began to pick up musical instruments, commencing with the flute and the violin. When he was eighteen, his choir master was crushed in a mine accident, and he was appointed to lead and teach the choir. "I studied up so as to be qualified, and did well and got a good choir, so obtained much credit."

Circumstances changed significantly when he was twenty, but there was little to diminish his confidence and personal optimism. He left his home because of differences with his parents, and he lost his girlfriend of seven years. There were some dark charges, which he denied, but while the total impact was severe enough to cause him to become "neglectful" of his church duties, he continued enthusiastically devoting his time to music. Severing his ties with the Mormons, he eventually married a Miss Harriet Foster at St. Peter's Church when he was twenty-one. His musical career expanded with engagements increasing almost daily. In his twenty-second year he made "another rapid stride, greater than all." He learned the trombone and the cornet and formed his first band, the Willenhall Rifle Corp Brass Band, with all members now enlisted under Queen Victoria:

> "I felt quite gay with always being the leading man of the band. My bright scarlet trimmings, and fine plume in my shako gave me quite a raise. The corp and the public encouraged and paid us well, this made me feel much better."

Despite his numerous musical successes, he still felt a certain need to return to Mormonism, and in 1862 when his wife on her own became involved with the Mormons, he was rebaptized and ordained to the office of an elder, an office higher than any he had held before. And although he now became possessed of "the spirit of gathering," a Mormon expression for leaving Europe for Utah, he continued to advance financially and socially in English society. He became a member of the Literary Institute, and his band was invited to perform at the Town Hall. In front of several important dignitaries, William Grant gave a short but impressive speech. In his words, he "was a popular man in all classes of society." Perhaps, the crowning achievement of his musical career in England was in 1865 when his company participated in the Grand Military Review at Warwick Castle. There were some 200 bands with some 30,000 men under the commander-in-chief of the British Army, the Duke of Cambridge.

Despite a successful career in England, William now wanted to leave England for the United States, but the American Civil War prevented him. Finally, in 1866, he and his family emigrated. And if we are to accept William's perspective of 1882, his time in Utah was simply an extension of his successes in England. After a short and somewhat unpleasant tenure in Salt Lake, a committee of four or five men invited him to move to American Fork and teach a brass band that was being newly formed. He made many friends, built a new home, and, after advice from his bishop, opened a music notation store in American Fork:

> "So I went home full of faith, took out of the pocket all the money I had--a one dollar greenback, laid it on the table, straightened it out, slapped it for good luck, talked to it, blessed it and prayed God this one dollar just going out into the world on speculation might be much blessed and grow, multiply into ten thousand."

And by 1872, he was able to write "Business, business. My brain was almost whirling with joy. Everybody seemed to be patronizing me."

William Grant's record of his first forty-four years is a priceless document, but from the point of view of characterization, it has serious limitations. While it reveals the character of Grant at the age of forty-four, it does not give us enough information to see Grant as a dynamic character. If we were to characterize him, we would have to see him as a very confident, optimistic man. There are signals here and there in his journal that indicate what will come later, but generally, the portrait we have of William Grant is static and nondeveloping. This is not to say that such a characterization would be bad or inaccurate; it is only to say that it reflects a man at one point in his life, a man who is not undergoing change.

However, if the keeper of the journal makes entries over a period of time, it is possible that the writer could have at his disposal material covering several changes in the subject's circumstances and reflecting several levels of personality development. The writer would then be able to develop a dynamic character. A personal tragedy may leave the journal writer bitter and lonely or with a developed level of empathy similar but also unlike anything he had had before the tragedy. His journal entries might give graphic details of this development, enough to allow the writer to show how events deeply affected and changed the subject. What is fascinating and really very moving about William Grant's journal begins to occur around 1880.

Apparently, William Grant had generally acted as the personal secretary to a certain George Rowley, a blind citizen of the community who had been both a musical friend to William as well as a valued customer. William had also for some time served as postmaster. Sometime in 1877, William Grant had observed some circulars addressed to George Rowley describing musical instruments, and William was angered both by the competition and George's lack of loyalty. William, supposing that George had no inkling of the mail he was receiving, tossed the circulars into the trash, but George was aware that William had received the circulars and began to press for William's removal as postmaster. Immediately rumors began to fly about other missing mail, and William was obliged to publish a document defending his entire tenure as postmaster. William was deeply hurt, and the loss of the postal contract impacted his business. His journal entry is significant: "it left me very weak however in the body and I drank more tea occasionally as a stimulant only."

William's business, however, picked up despite this setback, although as time passed, he began to complain increasingly of becoming "tired and weary with hard work and worry." It was in August of 1888 that he suffered a loss that seemed to alter signficantly his sense of optimism. After a large Sunday dinner, the total family, twenty-three in all, took a ride some three to five miles out to the lake. As can happen with uncharted lake bottoms, one of his sons dove into an area that was over his head and drowned, and it was not until the next day that they were able to recover the body. The father's description of the recovery is heart-breaking:

> "It was my son. I was glad to see his sweet face. Blood rushed from his mouth, and a wound was on the left side of his mouth. We

bore him gently to the wagon, wrapped him in two quilts and loaded up, started for home."

In his words, "this seemed the greatest affliction I had ever had and was a hard trial for us all."

A growing sense of despair began to characterize his journal. In 1889, he was sent a second time to prison for practicing polygamy, and the contrast between his attitude this time and his first brush with the law in 1884 is significant. The first arrest and time in prison had had all the air of a religious outing. Not so with the second. An inmate--apparently not in prison for religious reasons--committed suicide, and William heard him shout out after he had cut his own throat. By December, he was complaining of headaches and sickness and general ill treatment by the prison guards. For William the situation was now contributing to his growing depression. In October of 1890, he attended the church's general conference in Salt Lake City and voted to sustain the church leadership in abolishing polygamy, but this too left him confused and depressed:

> "Went to October conference. Saw many friends and it was an interesting time, as the great manifesto on polygamy was brought before the church. I heard it all but was mystified and cannot say I was pleased at all, though I held up my hand to agree that Pres. Woodruff should have the right to issue it and that I would not oppose it, but I hated it."

In March of 1891, he noted that "business is dull, and times are hard, and much sickness and death prevails." Gradually, he began to associate the decline in his business with disloyalty in his friends. His yearly summaries by 1892 were generally characterized by statements such as "trials and hardships." By June of 1894, he was complaining that "times are hard, and money is scarce. Debts are pressing and it is a terrible strain on my nerves." In December of 1895, the sheriff appeared at his door, and William found himself sued in court for failure to pay an overdue bill. A few days later during prayer, he collapsed into his wife's arms.

Despite the financial strain, William continued to be a popular and sought-after speaker and performer, particularly for church functions and funerals, and this seemed to give him the sense of personal esteem that he needed. In February, 1896, he recorded that George Teasdale, a high church official, laid his hand on his shoulder and called him "a pillar in the church, firm, true as a rock." Yet even here, William betrayed a certain insecurity and disharmony. A few months later, he recorded that he had "had much uphill work to meet, through the jealousy and envy of those who should sustain me, the ward authority looking down on me some, and doing several things detrimental to me and my happiness." Then in May 1897, one of his wives died, leaving him deeply depressed:

"We are still distressed, and often visit the grave of our departed one. It is again summer. A great sorrow again overtakes me. I am in debt all around and the Deseret News Co. has sued me and got judgment, and the sheriff comes to distress us for $291.44."

His growing estrangement now took on the tone of paranoia:

"I live among a strange people and have much to contend with that does not appear on the surface. I am fully certain that a strong influence is used against me, and my interests, and that from people who ought to be my first supporters."

Despite the fact that he was appointed purchasing agent in June of 1898 for the Sunday school, he was released the same month as organist, lamenting that "there were circumstances set around the case, obnoxious to me." One year later, he lost in a school election convinced that "the people look down on me, and do not wish me well." In January of 1900, he was awarded a badge for his service to the Sunday school, and his exultation was almost as poignant as his earlier sense of betrayal. One month later after having received the special badge, he was asked to resign from the Sunday school as his "business every Sunday morning of delivering papers all around" prevented him from doing his duty. His reaction is revealing:

"I have been almost ignored the past few years in the position, and really wished to get out of it as I have so much to do with my own family and business at home and have no regrets in the matter at all."

The year 1900 was a good business year for the sixty-two-year-old William, but his failing health and financial responsibilities continued to weigh him down. Then in January of 1901, there was an important church conference at which he received no "call," a Mormon expression for ecclesiastical office. In March of 1901, he lost his position in the ward choir to a "new man with new methods," and in February 1907, he wrote that "it is seldom that I am noticed for anything in a public way. Too old, I suppose, though I am often called to pray in the stand also to bless the sick, and make short addresses." In 1910, he made one of his last journal entries:

"Old age has enfeebled me. Being out of office has stopped many of my old time public duties and publicity. I am almost a nonentity so there is little to record."

William died six years later.

A characterization of William when he was forty-four would have been much different from a characterization of William shortly before his death. A dynamic or developing characterization would take this change into account while a static characterization would show William's character at a certain point and place in time. The writer of family history, however, normally does not have enough original material at his disposal to allow him to develop a dynamic characterization and usually can only present a static character--the William Grant, for example, of the age of forty-four or shortly before death. Either approach is, of course, valid although it is true that no human being ever was a static, nonchanging personality. William Grant of forty-four was not the William Grant of sixty or seventy. And at which point in time does the writer's portrait accurately reflect the historical subject? When does one sum up the totality of a human's life? There are no answers to these questions, but in the case of the family narrator, the issue is usually decided on the basis of available material. In family narration, the writer usually presents a character as it lies frozen in time, and the static characterization more often prevails over the dynamic.

Methods of Character Presentation. The three principal methods of characterization available to the family narrator are direct (or explicit) exposition, which some divide into physical description and personality analysis; the dialogue and/or thoughts of a character; and the use of action to depict the qualities of a character. In light of what we have been discussing about characterization, each method has its place and is in turn dictated by the kinds and amount of original material available. Before deciding which method or methods you plan to use, first establish the trait or basic quality on which you plan to focus. Normally the information at your disposal will dictate the trait or traits you want to emphasize; however, ultimately it is your decision, your creative judgment, that narrows down the basic character trait that is the focus of your characterization.

1: Characterization Through Direct (or Explicit) Exposition. Normally when dealing with a historical character about whom we have gleaned information from the traditional genealogical sources such as census and probate documents, the direct or explicit exposition is the commonly used method. It is definitely the easiest and is the same technique that we explored in Chapter 2: "Using Genealogical and Local History Records to Write the Historical Exposition." As in the description, the direct exposition of character begins with a dominant impression or theme with supporting details that bear out that basic idea.

It is often surprising what the writer does know about a historical figure. He may actually know physical details from a military record. He may have a listing from an inventory of the man's possessions at the time of death, which were probably a reflection of the subject's interests and even character. Censuses--often state censuses more than federal-- also contain surprising details about a family's physical possessions. We have already met Elisha Partridge who died in 1787 either while falling from his horse or while walking his horse near Union, Maine. The cause of death is given as apoplexy. When we turn to Elisha's inventory, a fascinating world of details opens up to us revealing much both about Elisha's and his wife Sarah's characters.

The wardrobe items listed indicate a man typical of other men of the period, particularly those living in towns. It would appear that Elisha possessed a variety of clothing in a variety of colors: a blue coat, a blue jacket, leather breeches, beaver hat, grey wig, shoes, blue and white stockings, leggings, and silver knee buckles and shoe buttons. Elisha was also literate. He could read and write: he owned spectacles and an inkstand, and he had a small library, which for the time and period would appear to be reasonably substantial: a Bible, hymnals, sermon books, a collection of Psalms, and a church platform. The fact that the inventory lists these as "old" might indicate that Elisha used these books or that he had inherited them; both conclusions seem reasonable. The kind of reading material also indicates a religiously inclined person. He was also self-sufficient. He owned a gun and probably used it for hunting purposes. He had nets for fowling, and he apparently fished for food. He raised potatoes, flax, corn, wheat, and turnips, and he had hogs, sheep, and cattle. He had tools such as a gimlet and awls for working woods. He also possessed scythes, pitchforks, and a log chain, the latter probably for pulling stumps. All these tools would indicate a physically capable man who, even if he were as overweight as he is depicted in Ben Ames Williams's *Come Spring,* was still able to pitch hay and pull stumps.

The inventory also gives us some idea as to what kind of a person his wife was. Weaving equipment would indicate that Sarah made much of their own cloth that she in turn probably fashioned into garments. She also had a well-developed kitchen: a brass warming pan and skimmer, funnel, cider keg, tea kettle, and piggens (pail). She had pewter dishes, pewter table spoons, knives and forks, two old butcher knives, a tea pot, and some pint basins. There was a valet for cups and saucers, a meal chest, a large cupboard, a washing tub, and some barrels. There were lancets for bleeding cattle, probably for medicinal purposes, but it is possible that Sarah may have used blood for certain dishes. She also used a toasting iron and a pair of scales. One could almost, with a little imagination, reconstruct the typical menus and dishes that Sarah prepared in her late 1700s kitchen.

Using the above information as well as the complete details of the inventory (see Chapter 2), let us try our hand at a direct exposition of these two people. Our basic thesis that Elisha and Sarah Partridge were typical, self-reliant settlers is as follows:

> Elisha and Sarah Partridge were typical of the unbending, self-reliant settlers who gathered along the coast of Maine from Massachusetts following the French and Indian War. Both were

religious, versed in the Bible and read in the tenets and concepts of their fortifying Puritan faith. Elisha, who could not only read but write, was given to the brief vanities of the city with his wig and silver buttons and buckles and most likely to financial indiscretions. At death he owed almost as much as he owned. Sarah, of simpler tastes, knew how to weave the cloth and fashion the clothing that she and her family needed, as well as to work the raw materials of frontier life into palatable foods and dishes. Elisha, who liked the more carnal pleasures of tobacco and cider, possessed the physical strength to work the untutored but beautiful land on the edge of the wilderness, pulling stumps and clearing fields, planting cereal crops, hunting the forests, fishing the streams and ponds, and raising and butchering livestock; and he knew how to provide some of the luxuries of life by working the hardwoods of the forests into beds, chests, valets, cupboards, and chairs.

This explicit exposition is clearly in accord with the facts of the inventory and, while lacking in much individual detail, it does give us some idea of what these two people were and did some two centuries ago. We have stated directly or explicitly a general or dominant personality quality and supported that dominant trait with details. It is also important to note that although we may find it interesting that both of these persons were self-reliant, it is the detail that holds our interest. For many writers of family history, direct exposition or exposition in general is the only honest way of writing about the family since narration, with its flights of fiction, causes the writer to fashion plots, conversations, and incidents that may bear out the general truth of a historical figure but are themselves actually products of the author's imagination. The point is, however, not how to avoid narration by using direct exposition but how to use direct exposition in narration. Generally, the longer the work, the easier it is for the author to include passages of direct exposition; however, with the short story, the author should limit direct exposition to a few sentences.

The following story is an example of narration that employs direct exposition. It has much in common with simple description (see Chapter 2), proceeding from a basic or dominant character trait. We do not hear the subject speak, nor do we enter into his mind or thoughts although we do see him in action. The narrator, in the first person with an all-seeing eye (omniscient point-of-view), presents the character alternating between direct exposition and action. (For a more complete discussion of point of view, see the section later in this chapter on point of view.) The sections of direct exposition are italicized:

Olin

In the very small town of Bluff, Utah, there was until recently an old man who sat on a bench on the front porch of his rock house, watching the cars as they drove by. He was so colorful, so rural American, and so predictably there, that he had become a favorite subject for camera buffs looking for memorabilia of their sojourn into the rugged West.

Years ago, I began to look for him as I drove through this hamlet, intrigued as others by his suspendered American Gothic appearance. Being an oral historian rather than a camera buff, it was only natural that sooner or later, I would want to make a verbal profile of this man who waited by the side of the road. I could not know, as I thought of capturing the thoughts and recollections of this old man, how very humble and yet profound they would be. Nor could I know what a message his life would hold for me personally, and for all of those who seek to understand the people of San Juan.

When I inquired as to the identity of this old man, my questions were answered with amusement, but also forthrightness by members of a community who long ago had learned to accept and, in their own way, protect the subject of my interest. *His name was Olin Oliver, I was told, and he was somewhat retarded. However, he had been in the community longer than anyone else, ·and could perhaps give some insights into the community's past.*

I was in the area at that time with a group of students from California State University, Fullerton, conducting an oral history project relating to life in southeastern Utah. The burdens of administering this project soon forced me to realize that I would not be able to conduct this oral history personally, so I sent one of my better students to do the recording. It was not until much later, while doing the final editing in preparation for printing these interviews, that I came to understand from Olin's own simple words and from the insights of others who had known and loved him, the layers of significance in the uncluttered story of his life.

Olin Oliver once had been a bright, venturesome boy, running along the sand banks of the San Juan River and climbing for cliff flowers in the rims surrounding Bluff. The whispering murmur of the river at night, the snuggling protectiveness of the sandstone cliffs, the bright patch of blue sky overhead by day, and the blanket of almost reachable stars at night lent security to a young life that had known its share of adversity before the family settled in Bluff. Nestled into the warmth of the setting, encouraged by the genuine friendliness of the people, and enchanted by the many choices for real adventure offered by his situation, *Olin became one of the most ebullient, exuberant partakers of nature's feast.* Then one evening, tragedy struck. Riding home quickly, after having been engrossed too long in some childish delight, Olin attempted to turn his horse too sharply out of the lane in front of his house, and the horse slipped and fell on the ice of a late fall storm. Olin's head struck on the protruding root of a locust tree.

Friends carried Olin's unconscious body to his home, where his mother called one of the two town midwives, the only medical authority available, to attend him while his uncle and a friend drove a borrowed car, then rode horseback the sixty miles to bring the nearest doctor from Cortez, Colorado.

When Doctor Johnson arrived a day and a half later, Olin was in a deep coma. Arranging a series of kerosene lanterns and mirrors so that he could adjust his available light, the doctor went to work immediately, opening the scalp, chipping out the crushed skull bone and dipping out the blood that had pooled against the brain. For most of the night the doctor worked, bending all the talent and effort he could give to this effort. Finally, just before dawn, the doctor's shoulders sagged, and he turned his tired body to face the equally exhausted midwife, who had attended him through the operation. Pointing out the extensive damage to the boy's brain, and the hopeless bleeding that continued, the doctor stated that regardless of anything they might do, the boy almost certainly would be dead within hours, and that should he live, his brain would be hopelessly impaired. Stating that he had left a critically ill patient in Colorado to come, he asked the midwife to explain to the family the hopelessness of the situation, then began picking up his surgical tools to leave. Almost as an afterthought, he left some strychnine tablets, telling the midwife that if Olin lived until morning, the family might give him one tablet each day to try to keep his tired heart going in the depths of his coma. Then Dr. Johnson was gone, to face the long ride back to Colorado and the exigencies that awaited him there.

The town's two midwives, family members and indeed the entire town watched over Olin during the next twenty-one days that he spent in the coma, prying open one corner of his locked mouth sufficiently to pour down his throat a few spoonfuls of broth each day, along with the strychnine tablet. *When he finally came out of the coma, he was paralyzed on one half of the body for an additional six weeks, and for the rest of his life, was deaf in one ear, blind in one eye, and lame in one leg. Olin did not die, thanks to the great effort of a country doctor, a village midwife, a loving family and an entire, concerned town, but his brain did suffer extensive damage, and this once bright boy was transformed into a person for whom every act of coordinating muscles and nerves and mind was an effort.*

As those long, trying years of childhood merged into the lonely years of adulthood, *Olin Oliver stood the gentle taunts of unthinking peers who never really meant to hurt, accepting in his simple way the role cast for him and relishing the acts of friendship accorded by many members of the community.* One of those friends was the village midwife who had wrestled with angels for his life, and saw in his simple existence the verities of mortality. When, in her eighties, she was almost forcibly removed to a nearby community to be cared for by her daughters, much of her sense of loss was caused by being separated from people such as Olin, whom she had always felt needed her in Bluff.

For Olin himself, life eventually provided a measure of compensation. As he lived his simple, uncomplicated existence, fighting his major battles with the fog that shrouded his brain and bound his muscles, he was kept from the weightier problems that pressed ever heavier on the shoulders of his peers. One by one his associates who earlier had mocked his infirmities became casualties of their own, one blown to bits in a mine accident, another killed in a car that failed to negotiate a curve, another living for many years as a veritable slave to a bottle of alcohol. There came a day when stress or danger or fatigue had exacted its toll, and few remained of that generation which had once raced carefree along the sand banks of the San Juan. *In old age, when most people's minds become soft and fog-shrouded, Olin's mind gained no more cobwebs than it had before. There finally came a day when his simple dignity would give him a bearing that would stop the cars of passing tourists, and his thick humor, incongruous when he was 35, was now accepted gleefully.*

Olin Oliver waited long to make much of a contribution to others beyond that of the example of a happy, uncomplicated perpetual youth, smiling uncomplainingly at the vagaries of a twisted fate. But as an old man sitting on his bench, Olin brightened the day for hundreds, both acquaintances and casual passersby, compelled to stop by the magnetic attraction of a little boy who got to be an old man thanks to the second mile effort of a country doctor, a village midwife, and a concerned community.

(Gary Shumway)

There is much that needs to be reemphasized. First, direct exposition is the technique in which the author directly tells us what he wants us to know about the subject. But important to the success of the technique itself is the principle of dealing with details and events of high emotional intensity or what we have also termed significant details or events. Olin's life involved thousands of insignificant hours sitting on the porch of his rock house. Correctly so, the author has chosen to ignore all of these and to deal only with those details and events of emotional intensity that make his basic point. The author has so totally immersed himself in the details of this small town and in the lives of the people who lived in this town that he cannot help but provide us with a moving and winning characterization.

2: Characterization Through Thoughts and Dialogue. Many writers such as Ernest Hemingway use a technique known as dramatic dialogue in which the author relies largely on dialogue to present character or delineate personality patterns. The narrator simply puts the reader in time and place, and the characters of the story, through dialogue, carry the story from there. The technique has much to commend itself, after all, what we say is a reflection of what we think and feel. The problem for the family historian is that we seldom if ever have access to what our ancestors said much less thought, and even if we can reasonably reconstruct thinking and speaking patterns from personal sources such as a journal or letters, we still have no way of establishing that anything like the reconstructed dialogue took place. For family history, characterization through thoughts and dialogue remains a controversial approach; those who accept Truman Capote's concept of "history as a novel" or Wallace Stegner's reconstruction of dialogue on the basis of slight circumstantial evidence will have no qualms about reconstructed dialogue while those who argue vehemently for absolute historical accuracy will settle for nothing less than verifiable quotations thus effectively rendering any dialogue in the family narrative impossible. For those in the latter category, characterization through direct or explicit exposition is the only acceptable method. The choice is the writer's although I will proceed on the assumption that there are those who feel free, on the basis of slight historical evidence, to fabricate reasonably accurate dialogue and thoughts as a means of revealing character.

Good dialogue does not happen by accident; it requires careful observation. Writing textbooks normally give the advice that it is only through honing one's listening skills that the writer can arrive at accurate and natural dialogue. Each individual has his own speaking patterns as well as patterns that vary according to the mood or circumstances, and it is really impossible to write natural and credible dialogue without hearing what people normally say. Obviously, the basic rule is that the dialogue must sound real or be natural, not fabricated. But how does one go about hearing dialogue and thought patterns, for example, from a century ago?

There is probably no one in a better position to establish reasonable dialogue and thought patterns than the family researcher. After all, he more than anyone else is intimately familiar with the original documents dating from the time and period, the social class and the interest background of his narrative subject, and he more than anyone else knows what is appropriate or reasonably correct. Most writing textbooks, though, counsel against reproducing on a whole-scale basis the thought and speech patterns of a distant region or time, particularly on reproducing regional dialects in dialogue. Wallace Stegner in his *Recapitulation* relies essentially on two or three words to establish the German-English dialogue of one of his characters: "vot," "dot," and "ja." The rest of his speech patterns are essentially colloquial English. Literal dialect transcriptions only serve to confuse, and they really add little if anything. The subtle distinctions between regional dialects may warm the heart of the linguist, but most readers do not care. The trick is to lift

that which is significant from the historical documents and that which
gives the flavor of the dialogue of the region and time without bogging
down the reader with confusing transcriptions. C. Hugh Holman, William Thrall, and Clarence Hibbard in their *Handbook to Literature* (New
York: Odyssey, 1960) express it perhaps as well as anyone: the trick is to
give "the impression of naturalness without being an actual, verbatim
record of what may have been said, since fiction as someone has explained, is concerned with 'the semblance of reality,' not with reality itself." What then is "the semblance of reality"?

The one thing that more than anything else contributes to this
"semblance" is vocabulary. Most people simply used different words for
things in the past or used words that we today use with a slightly different meaning. And most of these vocabulary items are close enough to
what we say today to allow us to "get it" without a lot of footnoting, although some footnotes will obviously at times be necessary. Thomas
Wells, writing in 1862 through 1864 in the midst of the Civil War, uses
words that most of us can reasonably guess at. For the more obscure
terms, the reader is referred to the *Oxford English Dictionary*. At one
point Wells threatens to take a "french furlow" because he is tired of
fighting for "these fig Officers." It does not take much imagination for us
to establish what either of these expressions refers to although I venture
that few today have heard or used these terms. He has "a plenty of good
vituals to eat" which not only illustrates peculiar vocabulary but also an
unusual syntax that may represent the speaker more than it does the
time and region. Still, syntax is just as important as vocabulary and normally as easily understood by the reader. The family narrator should
keep a notebook with distinctive and characteristic phrases that he can
refer to when constructing dialogue; keeping lists, or "listing" as some
teachers of creative writing courses term it, is actually a good process of
understanding how someone spoke. As an example, I have listed below
several expressions lifted from Thomas Wells's letters defining the more
obscure terms and preserving the original spelling, which illustrate both
the peculiar terms as well as syntax that this man used:

-a little fight with the rebs
-to guard a wagon train through
-when will this miserable war come to a close
-I hardly believe it
-I hate thoes copperheads [northern sympathizers with the south]
-our boats wer runing by Vicksburg
-the darkest hour is just before day
-it is a money making cheam, and a rotton consurn [affair]
-I would like to get a paper [letter] firstrate [immediately]
-they did not get there untill long in the night
-I was determined to stick it through if I could
-I took a does of pills
-the gunboats throed a lot of shell in amongst them and made them

skidadle
-I was unwell and hardly able to get a round
-I never ait a mouth full of anything untill night
-it commenced raining
-in the night the wind changed in to the north
-we lay warm as minks
-I sent it by a fellow in Company C
-the boys are washing considerable this weak
-Oscar is fat as a bare
-everthing here is very dear [expensive]
-last Sunday some one hooked [stole] a gold pin that I payed $1.50 cents
for in Rockford
-bulley for the draft
-I hate thoes Coperheads . . . worse than a secesh [secessionist] of the
south
-the rebs calculated to pitch on to us this week wednesday
-I had to lay by my writing untill now
-everything went off quietly and pleasantly untill about 11 oclock
-Cousin Henry was taken sick sudenly last Thursday noon
-I am hartily ashamed to send you so short a letter
-I had a bully good supper of buiscuit and milk
-I invited him to take dinner with
-I have plenty of good vituals to eat
-I hav not a terible sight of strength yet
-I hav a very lame back
-I cant make it seem that she is dead
-the row of barracks caught a fire
-I dont want to go around in the mud

Although no one can ever be sure that Thomas Wells actually spoke as he wrote, it is reasonable for the writer to proceed to reconstruct speech patterns with some of these items, thus giving the "semblance" of dialogue truth. But the writer must be careful not to overstate his case. Remember the key word is "semblance." Irving Stone, in his introduction to *The President's Lady*, elects specifically not to emulate the flowery speech patterns of a former era but instead to write his dialogue in simpler English, "striving constantly to make certain that the difference is one of words, and never of thought, feeling or meaning." The author must be careful not to overwhelm the reader with unusual speech patterns and elaborate phonetic transcriptions, yet the reader should come away from the dialogue feeling that he has heard Thomas Wells speak. This technique depends for its success on the existence of original documents, and the writer may often be forced to use contemporary sources to develop a person's dialogue when there is little or nothing that has survived with the peculiar vocabulary and syntax of the subject of the narrative.

With the technique clearly in mind, there are some rules that the writer should observe:

1. Remember that people have always operated on different wave lengths. No one statement means the same thing to all people, since each person interprets another's words with the bias of his own experiences and concerns. To give the "semblance of truth," it is important to recognize that historical persons had different frames of reference than we do, and good characterization requires that the writer try to reflect these peculiar and, to us, "illogical" historical biases.

2. Avoid dialogue that wanders. Remember that we are attempting to characterize through dialogue, not wander aimlessly through a complete transcript. If the dialogue does not serve to develop a character, it is best ended. Remember, as family narrators we are already on questionable ground by using dialogue; why increase a sense of distrust if the dialogue serves no purpose.

3. Make sure that the dialogue is not an extension of our own modern speech or thought patterns or like everyone else's in the story. Each person should have his own peculiar style or dialogue although it will be difficult to determine each particularly if the writer is dealing with only one set of source documents. Here, the best approach is careful historical listening.

4. Do not mix the dialogue patterns of one region or time period with the patterns of another region or time period. It is maddening but almost predictable that beginning writers of the family narrative will insist on mixing, for example, the patterns of the rural, Maine settler with the patterns of the Bostonian Puritan. After all, they are all quaint, and from a distance they sound reasonably alike. Once again, if the writer has considered his source documents carefully, he should have no trouble.

5. Consider the perennial argument about the attributive phrase "he said/she said." If one establishes two characters in a dialogue, it is not necessary to repeat "he said" or "she said" after each statement; it is sufficiently clear to the reader who is speaking. If it is not clear who is speaking, you may want to consider synonyms for "said" to indicate speakers although I have seen too many beginning writers become so clever describing how a character says something that they tax the reader mentally. Maybe it is simply easier to use "said," "asked," and "answered" or at least reasonable and straight-forward synonyms.

The following student story is essentially a characterization of an elderly Danish couple who have been called upon to bury Uncle Knut in the small Mormon town of Fayette, Utah. The author has avoided littering the dialogue with Danish-American colloquialisms and grammatical inaccuracies, yet there is enough in the story to remind us that these are Americans who have not entirely left behind their ties with the old country. The emphasis is on the characters of the Grandmother, or Besta (from the Danish "Bestamor" or grandmother), and Grandfather and on the relationship between the two. While there is direct exposition of character, most of the characterization is advanced through dialogue. I have italicized those parts of the dialogue which bear on the two characters:

Uncle Knut's Coffin

I'm sure Besta and Grandpa were saddened and shocked at Uncle Knut's untimely death, but they were from old country stock and not given to a show of feelings. They were used to hard times and disappointments. Besta lost four of her children before they reached their first birthdays, and Grandpa had seen two of his brothers perish at sea when they were washed overboard of their fishing vessel. Now their hardy souls were bent on weaving a strong fabric of life here in the new country, and they had not much time for tears.

Now at 48, *struck down in the "prime of life,"* as Besta lamented, he lay in our front room parlour awaiting the ministrations of Brother Jensen, who it appeared had no wood to build him a coffin to accommodate his 6-foot, 7-inch frame.

Uncle Knut made his home with us when he arrived in this country from Denmark. He was named for one of the early Vikings and had grown into a remarkable physical copy of the ancient ruler. His flaming red hair and beard were the first things that arrested attention, together with his massive frame.

"I want you should get him out of here and down to the undertaker's today," said Besta as she wiped her hands on her apron and looked nervously at Uncle Knut resting on her best parlour sofa.

"Well, Brother Jensen said he expected a new shipment of lumber today and he could get a coffin built by tomorrow," Grandpa assured her. He was used to dealing with Besta's fretting over what he called "small details." But in this case it was no small matter, with Uncle Knut draped over the red sofa, legs bent at the knees over the end, his size 13 boots dragging on Besta's flowered carpet.

In life, he would not have dared to venture into Besta's parlour unless we had company, and even then, he didn't sit on the sofa, but on an old chair that groaned under his weight but somehow remained intact.

In death his countenance was one of complete repose, and I thought I could even detect the trace of a smile. Besta could no longer scold him for coming into her house with muddy boots or for lying on her best velvet sofa.

Besta set about placing small pillows under the craggy head and tried to rearrange the brawny arms over his chest.

"It just isn't right for a body to be dead on my sofa. He should've died in his bed like any normal person," she complained.

"Well, if he wasn't so tall, we could have had services today,"

Grandpa said. *"You know as well as I do, Knut just won't fit into a regular coffin. Brother Jensen always keeps two at the ready, but they won't do us any good for Knut."*

"I still say he should've been more considerate and died in his own bed," Besta continued grumbling. Just how a man could determine when and how he was going to die did not seem to concern her. *"And another thing. He hasn't got any decent buryin' clothes like he should've had. Always spending his money on 'spirits' and women. Never could save a dime that way."* Her hands kept going nervously to her face and neck, trying to catch a few stray wisps of hair and tuck them into place. *"He'll just have to be buried in the clothes he is wearing."*

It was true that Uncle Knut liked his "spirits" and bragged he could "drink any man under the table" and still manage to navigate his way home in the small country town where we lived. He was also very handy with the women, and while he romanced several widows in Fayette, he could never be snared into marriage by any one of them, although several had tried. Everyone was well aware of his faults, but he had the redeeming trait of being loved by most of the children around. I can remember being carried by him, tossed into the air and caught by those giant hands, then placed on his shoulder while he pranced around the room singing a Danish sea chantey.

Now his great heart had stopped while he was imbibing at the local bar just on the outskirts of the Mormon town. He was carried home by four of his buddies and placed on Besta's sofa, because they could not manage to hoist him up the steep narrow steps to his loft bed.

Besta brought a basin of water and towels into the parlour and began washing Uncle Knut's hands and face, although there was little of his face to wash since the beard covered most of it.

Our town boasted a large building which housed the livery stable at one end, the barber and undertaker on the other end, with the general store in the middle. While Brother Jensen furnished plain wood coffins for the town folks, it was usually up to the women of the church to prepare the deceased for burial in the little weed-grown cemetery at the edge of town.

Around 10 o'clock that morning Brother Jensen arrived at our front door with horse and wagon to take Uncle Knut down to his place of business.

"Don't know why they didn't take him there in the first place," Besta said. *"Wasn't any use bringing him here."*

"Brother Tollefson said they thought he was just passed out," Grandpa said. "They didn't know his heart had stopped."

The only doctor we could call lived in a town 10 miles away, and folks didn't call him in the middle of the night unless it was a serious illness, or a baby about to be born, much less for a man presumed to have passed out from too much drink.

Brother Jensen brought along the two Tollefson brothers, and together with Grandpa, they carried Uncle Knut out to the wagon and then proceeded down to the undertaking parlour.

I watched them go, and wondered about death like most children, but since I had not had experience with death of anyone close, the real impact of his dying did not penetrate my inner feelings, and I did not cry. Looking back, I realize I fully expected him to again appear at our door and in his booming voice call out, "Where's that scalawag of a kindlein to bring me my slippers." I usually ran for them, then hid behind a big chair while he pretended to hunt for me.

The day grew warmer as noon came, and Grandpa said no lumber had arrived for Brother Jensen. Around 1 o'clock he came over and advised Grandpa that the roads above Stringtown had been washed out by the spring floods and there would be no lumber delivered for at least a week. While a man on horseback could get through, no wagon could make it.

Besta paused at the table where she was working bread dough, her hands in midair covered with flour and dough. She looked at Grandpa over her glasses, her black eyes more penetrating than usual. *"You mean Knut is still without a coffin?"* she asked.

"Well, he can't be kept much longer, the weather turning warm and all, although Brother Jensen said maybe we could put him in Sister Lingle's ice house for a couple of days."

Grandpa put his old hat on the peg by the stove and sat down heavily in a chair near the table by Besta. She went on kneading the bread dough, saying nothing, but I could tell she was thinking plenty.

After the midday meal, Grandpa went back down to Brother Jensen's, and when he came home later he said services for Uncle Knut would be held the next morning in the town meeting house. Since he wasn't considered to be much of a Christian, he would not be buried by the church.

Besta looked at Grandpa with her face fixed in a scowl. *"What is he being buried in if Brother Jensen couldn't build him a coffin?"* she asked.

Grandpa looked very uncomfortable and fidgeted in his chair. *"We took care of things. Don't you worry none,"* he said. I could tell Besta was far from satisfied, but Grandpa went out to feed the stock, leaving her to ponder the situation.

The following morning at the town meeting house, people put in an appearance for the services, and I sat with Besta and Grandpa on the first row. There in front on a platform was a pine coffin, and as far as I could see, it was the same size as the one I had seen for old Mrs. Bonner who had died recently.

I could see that Besta was clearly puzzled as she kept looking at Grandpa and then back at the coffin. As soon as we got into the wagon at the cemetery to come home, I knew Besta would start again on Grandpa.

"*All right, what did you do?*" *she demanded.* Grandpa slapped the reins against old Jacob to get him going.

"*Why don't you just let things ride and don't bother yourself about it,*" *he said.*

"Because I want to know," Besta persisted.

Grandpa looked over at me, and I could tell it was one of those things he didn't want me to hear, but Besta was not to be put aside.

"*We sawed off his legs at the knees and laid them along side of him,*" *he finally said.* "*There just wasn't any other way as it is getting too warm to keep him any longer. Sister Lingle wouldn't have him in her ice house. Said he was a sinner and I guess she was afraid some of it would rub off on her.*"

I had seldom seen Besta without sufficient word power, but now she just stared straight ahead, speechless. In my child's mind, I too wondered and felt horror. Would God give Uncle Knut new legs when he got to Heaven?

(Vaneta Wolfe)

The dialogue reveals a very determined, directing Besta with a somewhat evasive, person-pleasing Grandpa. Certainly, the direct character analyses are an important part of understanding the two characters, but the dialogue, without confusing the reader with complicated transcriptions, does a good deal to delineate these two very different Danish-Americans's personalities. One may still argue for a dialogue that represents more accurately the dialect of the historical subjects. John Galsworthy's short story "Quality" is an example of just such an attempt: "Id is an Ardt" for "It is an art"; or "beople do nod wand good boods, id seems" for "people do not want good boots, it seems." However, most readers today do not want the challenge of such a complicated dialogue. They would probably agree with Irving Stone who, in his introduction to *The President's Lady*, announces that the language of his historical subjects was "more flowery and formal," and that he chose instead to use in his "re-created" dialogue "simpler English."

3: Characterization Through Action. The final method of characterization is through action, not just any action but significant action, action that helps us to see and understand the basic trait on which the author has chosen to focus. There is the story reported in Sibley's *History of the Town of Union* about how Elisha Partridge, one moonlit night while "paddling up the river above Round Pond," encountered an old bear "munching acorns on the point of land on the east side." He whistled for Sambo, a neighbor's dog whose kennel was not far distant, and Sambo ran "furiously down to the river, and at the first bound" jumped "half-way across the channel" succeeding in treeing the animal in a pine tree. They watched the bear until morning "when he was found to be very large, and to have climbed only about twenty feet from the ground. He was fired at. The ball struck him in the breast, but too low to wound the heart. Bruin then went up the tree about sixty feet. He was fired at and wounded several times. Finally, a ball was shot through his heart. He fell dead to the ground, breaking and clearing every limb in his way." And there is the probate inventory with its mention of grey wrapper, leggings, gun and powder horn, and spectacles. Certainly not much to allow the writer to single out a basic personality trait and to construct a story focusing on that trait, but let us follow the direct character exposition which we developed from the probate inventory of Elisha Partridge as the resourceful and self-reliant settler who was capable of dealing with almost any situation. Here I have italicized action that bears out this basic personality trait:

It was still early spring, and the ponds were not entirely free of ice. The moon's rays reflected brightly on the open but windy waters of Seven Tree Pond as Elisha Partridge nosed his leaky boat onto the hillock-protected stream that joined Seven Tree Pond with the smaller Round Pond. *He followed for some two miles the winding stream that provided a welcomed respite from the fierce winds that ranged in from the ocean over the large, open ponds of coastal Maine and entered Round Pond just above its forest-lined western shore. The wind again bit into his face, and he readjusted his heavy grey wrapper to cover his leather leggins. Moving out onto the pond, he strained his eyes against the uniform blackness of the northern shore to make out the point where still another stream led off through the marshy lowlands toward his one-room cabin.* Unexpectedly, the wind died. The time had past when the crackling ice on the pond sent forth rumblings through the night, and as he turned his boat in the sudden silence directly at the northern shore, *Elisha tuned his ear to every sound of the night and focused his eyes to catch any movement on the land.*

As he edged his boat into the mouth of the narrow stream, he passed the spot where several hapless women had drowned the previous spring when their overloaded and leaky boat had unexplainedly keeled over. People in the nearby settlements were able to hear their screams, but they had arrived too late to save anyone. *Elisha slipped his paddle in and out of the water annoyed that each time the paddle struck the water it broke the silence of the marsh. As he approached the point where the stream turned sharply to the left leaving the marshy area for higher and wooded ground, he caught a glimpse of something on the now northern side of the stream. For some reason, whatever it was, it was completely unaware of Elisha's approach. Now he held the paddle still, letting the water drip like thunder onto the surface of the slow-moving stream. His muscles taut, he failed to realize that instead of turning to the left he was headed straight for land, when suddenly he recognized the large shape as a bear munching acorns. He dropped his fingers to the bottom of the boat and felt carefully for his rifle and powder horn that lay in the dampness of the keel. He couldn't tell, but his instinct told him that his powder was wet and the rifle was useless.*

It was too late, his small boat had already struck land with a noise that awoke the intimidating silence of the night. Startled, the bear stopped, reared up on its hind legs, and took a long look in Elisha's direction.

Instantly, Elisha remembered Jason Ware's dog Sambo. Just last season Sambo had helped his master kill thirteen bears. *Placing his two fingers to his mouth, Elisha whistled as loudly as he could for Sambo whose kennel was not far away.* The bear resenting Elisha's intrusion into his world dropped down on all four and began to move toward Elisha. *Elisha furiously struck the paddle on the water, hoping to frighten the bear, but the noise only served to anger him.* Just then, Sambo bounded out onto the edge of the stream, circling and biting at the bear. Whenever the bear turned back on the dog, Sambo would beat a strategic retreat and then renew the attack. *As Elisha watched in the cold of early spring, Sambo drove the bear back up from the edge of the stream and up a pine tree.*

Elisha waited only long enough to be certain that the bear was going to stay up the tree, pushed his boat back into the stream and continued the remaining hundred or so yards to his cabin. When the first light of morning appeared, Elisha returned to find the bear still in the tree with Sambo barking and snarling at the base. As Sambo continued his barking, Elisha now cradled his rifle in the bend of a tree limb and fired directly at the animal. He aimed the first ball too high, but the second entered the bear's heart, and as he fell some sixty feet to the ground, he broke and cleared every limb in his way. Saying nothing, Elisha turned back toward his cabin.

From all of the stories in this section, it is obvious that no writer need use one method of characterization exclusively. The writer may emphasize dialogue as in the story about the Danish Uncle Knut, description and direct exposition as in the story about Olin, or action as in the story about Elisha Partridge, but each of these stories blends at least two and sometimes three of the methods of characterization. The most successful characterization is a mixture of all three. There is one technique, however, that all methods have in common. The writer through careful research establishes something unique or different in the character he is presenting, and through his characterization he plays up that unique quality. It may be a unique phrase, a physical attribute, or something about his personality. But ultimately what will result in a memorable character is that special uniqueness; and the writer should examine the historical data carefully to determine just what that might be.

THE PLOT

We have spent a good deal of time discussing patterns and basic personality traits. Isolating character or personality traits, as we have seen, is really the first step in characterization, and once we have a character or more properly a characterization, we are ready to set that character in action. Because it is impossible to think of a person except as *doing* or *being*, in other words in *action*, the action flows naturally out of the characterization although there is nothing to dictate that the process cannot work in reverse: starting first with action and then working back to a definition of the character or characters. Patterns, ways of understanding or interpreting basic source documents, lead us to conclude or conceptualize a basic premise or theme about the character or family, which we then work out in the form of a sequence of events or plot. The blending of the characterization and the plot is the narrative.

Establishing the Basic Theme. In Chapter 2: "Using Genealogical and Local History Records to Write the Historical Exposition," we established how we can recognize and distill basic patterns about the family from original source documents. We looked at family origins and settlement patterns, earning and spending patterns, value systems, and social and personality patterns, and we concluded that there are just about as many ways of looking at and interpreting the basic documents as there are people and families. Establishing patterns is the necessary first step in writing the family history--exposition or narrative--not because it is the source of good and clever ideas, but because ultimately we are attempting to tell the truth or explain what really did happen to someone in the past. For example, let us assume that the source documents show, as they did in the case of Christian Trapp, a high level of occupational instability. A story about occupational instability would not be a story; it would be a historical exposition. But if we develop a basic theme or premise about Trapp's occupational history, something to the effect that his personality or, to be more exact, his irrational temper, led to his constant dismissal from job after job, we have a basic premise or theme about which we can build a narrative. Such a premise is an extension of Trapp's characterization because it shows Trapp's flawed character in action.

Writers of good fiction seek constantly for that premise which distinguishes a story of quality from a story of maudlin sentimentality. And so should the writer of the family narrative. A theme that expresses the idea that the family's obstacles and struggles bring the family closer or that a person's faith in God overcomes all earthly ills and problems is simply not a realistic theme or for that matter a theme of quality. Most of the family narratives I have read fail on this basis alone: the author cannot accept the premise that his mother was anything but an angel or that his family was comprised of anyone but men and women of exemplary character and motivation who devoted their lives to countless acts of Christian mercy. I have already pointed out how members of my family for years preferred to ignore the fact that someone in our family history was hanged for rape. People might joke about a horse thief, but they do not joke about a rapist. The student that in her series of poetic-prose portraits showed her father as a violent, child molester and her mother as a passive contributor was a senior citizen before she could bring herself to write about her family. It is difficult to face the truth about ourselves or our families, but those who insist that the mistakes of the past should be forgotten and swept under the rug of maudlin sentimentality do not make good writers of family history. Let us establish clearly that a theme that ignores the truth about the past may save a family's honor, but it will never result in a quality narrative.

What is the theme or premise then that sets the historical character in an action that is more than maudlin sentimentality and leads to a quality narrative? The answer is not an easy one although the number of possible plot variations or basic themes is limited. Several years ago, Georges Polti wrote *The Thirty-Six Dramatic Situations* (translated by Lucille Ray, Boston: The Writer, Inc., 1986) in which he categorized all the basic plots in existence, and he challenged the reader to come up with any other kinds or types. Space does not permit detailing all thirty-six "dramatic situations." Even a summary of the basic idea of the thirty-six plots is overwhelming, but it is possible without doing too much violence to Polti's original "dramatic situations" to include most of his situations under something like fourteen basic plot themes. These thematic summaries obscure much of the conflict that Polti wrote into his original thirty-six "situations," but, for the purposes of our approach, the fourteen basic plot themes are a good place to begin a discussion of plot construction. As you consider each category, consider how you can translate each into a plot that deals with one of your families or family members.

> Plot Theme I: dealing with a threat
> Plot Theme II: taking vengeance or being pursued in
> vengeance
> Plot Theme III: overcoming or not overcoming an obstacle
> Plot Theme IV: seizing something or someone
> Plot Theme V: solving or not solving a problem
> Plot Theme VI: being in a position of rivalry with a relative
> Plot Theme VII: confronting a catastrophic circumstance
> Plot Theme VIII: making a sacrifice for an ideal, a relative, or
> a passion
> Plot Theme IX: competing with a superior individual
> Plot Theme X: being so much in love that one commits a
> crime, loves an enemy, or finds one's love dishonored or
> thwarted
> Plot Theme XI: being confronted with an obstacle to one's
> personal ambition

Plot Theme XII: making a terrible mistake that results in
   pain to someone else
Plot Theme XIII: suffering remorse for a crime
Plot Theme XIV: losing or recovering someone

You might consider these basic ideas as a start for analyzing and constructing plots. As you read, attend plays and movies, or watch television, list the plots that appeal to you or fall under the general categories of threat, revenge, overcoming, seizing, solving, familial rivalry, catastrophic circumstances, sacrifice, unequal rivals, love, ambition, mistakes, remorse, and losing. Try a few on for size in your family history. Some will work, some will not. And adapting one or several to your family history will naturally suggest others. Avoid, however, any cliche that would result in a trite plot. Finally, consider Polti's book.

There is, however, the important ingredient of conflict. (See the section later in this chapter on conflict.) It is fashionable today to see plot as an interplay of two opposing forces, and most understand these two opposing forces as coming in four basic types: man against another man; man against himself, or an aspect of one man's nature in conflict with another aspect of his personality; man against a group or society; and man against nature. If we now refer back to the fourteen basic plot ideas, we see how many of those listed involve one or more of the four conflicts. A threat may come from another person, nature, or from a man's own personality. The solving of a problem, the taking of vengeance, the overcoming of an obstacle, the seizing of something or someone, a catastrophic circumstance, a family rivalry, the sacrificing for an ideal, relative, or passion, the act of falling in love, the lure of ambition, a terrible mistake, suffering for a crime, and losing or recovering someone could all involve man against himself, another man, society, or nature.

But fitting general or basic categories such as "ambition" and "vengeance" with conflict is still too abstract to be of much use. Keeping in mind the several people we have met and the various patterns we have isolated about these individuals, let me suggest some plots that we could develop into narratives. For each plot idea, I have used one of the basic plot themes listed above as well as specified the exact conflict:

Plot Theme III (overcoming or not overcoming an obstacle): Christian
   Trapp's personal drive to provide for his family through maintaining
   well-paying jobs was overcome by his inability to get along with his
   co-workers--man against himself and man against society.
Plot Theme V (solving or not solving a problem): Elisha Partridge's
   self-reliant nature enabled him to overcome physical danger--man
   against nature.
Plot Theme VII (confronting a catastrophic circumstance): Joseph
   Farrow's timid personality made him incapable of dealing with the
   hostile world of loyalist Prince Edward Island--man against himself
   and man against society.

Plot Theme IX (competing with a superior individual): Thomas Wells's
controlling nature set him at odds with his sister--man against man
or woman.

Plot Theme XI (being confronted with an obstacle to one's personal ambition): William Grant's need for personal glory brought him to social ostracism--man against man and man against society.

This is not to say that these plots are final or complete. Obviously
they may also represent the author's mental preoccupations more than
the proper interpretation of the information. But they all illustrate that
a plot idea or theme fitted with the all-important ingredient of conflict
can lead to a plot. Generally, the more specific the theme and the conflict, the more workable the plot.

The following piece of writing, "Grandpa's '24 Chevy," is really a set
of instructions in how to set a character in action or, in other words, how
to distill a plot from a mass of data, in this case an account ledger. It im-
plies a narrative in which a very precise Grandpa fell hopelessly and ex-
travagantly in love both with a car and a lady but was thwarted by age in
fulfilling his ambitions (plot theme III: overcoming or not overcoming an
obstacle--man against himself). It is further an excellent example of listing or the preparing of lists of the basic elements or scenes in the plot
before one undertakes the writing of the narrative. The author intended
it as a finished product, and it is; but it is not a narrative. In some ways,
the genealogical purist might feel that the piece as it appears below is
enough--nothing else need be added or changed. The author has quite
correctly inferred a romance and really elaborated not one whit on the
basic information. Yet the exposition below is an excellent example of
what the process of listing might well be as a step in the process in constructing a narrative about Grandpa's romantic escapade in a '24 Chevy.
The steps, then, are as follows:

1. Examine the basic documents and isolate a pattern of events of
emotional intensity: here we note a series of expenditures indicating
what are, for Grandpa, irrational and unusual activities.

2. Develop a characterization of Grandpa detailing his loneliness,
his habit of making precise financial entries, his feisty independence,
and his declining physical abilities.

3. Through listing details, develop a plot idea or a plot theme:
Grandpa in losing his very precise head over a lady in one last glorious
fling encounters the unmovable obstacle of age. The conflict involves
one man's need for companionship being overcome by the severe personal limitations of age.

Grandpa's '24 Chevy

A yellow snapshot of a shiny black automobile, square as a box,
slid from the brittle pages of my grandfather's ledger, "Accts. 1924,
1907 Washington Blvd." As I studied the picture, a dozen memories

crossed my mind. An unsmiling Grandpa, erect in his high-collared shirt and narrow, black suit, held open the rear door of his newly acquired "Chivolett" like St. Peter attending the gates of heaven.

I could hear him speaking, "Come girls, mustn't be late on the first day of school. Grandpa drove all the way from Chicago to take you in his new car. Not every girl gets a ride to school."

"But does Daddy have to take our pictures?" from me, an impatient ten-year-old.

"Of course, honey. Doesn't he always on the first day of school?"

There was the flurry of setting up the camera on the tripod. Dad kept popping out from under the black cloth to adjust the three spindly legs and to rearrange us, while Grandpa removed a speck from the windshield with saliva and a grimy handkerchief. We froze to the count of five, sighed with relief at having recorded one more moment in family history, and began the lurching, perilous, six-block journey to school.

But why was this particular snapshot in the account book instead of Grandpa's family album? For a clue I leafed through crumbling blue- and red-lined pages that were filled with the daily problems of operating his rooming house.

The first few months were a dreary list of expenses: calcimine, wallpaper, bedbug powder, underwear, light bulbs, gas bills, and a constant "ad for housekeeper." Then, during April, alien items appeared.

Reading through the next nine months, I discovered entries which told a tale of frustration and possibly a small romance, a hitherto unknown segment of Grandpa's lonely existence.

It all began innocently:

1924

Repair garage roof	$14.00
Cement alley	$12.00
New garage doors	$70.00
Garage lock	$2.89

Since, according to receipts, his rooms rented for $8 and $10 a month, the above represented a tremendous outlay to the frugal man. However, the last item in April explained his extravagance: "Ad for auto--$2.70."

Then, on May 1st: "Chevrolet Sedan--$550."

How Grandpa's blue eyes must have gleamed as he made that entry! And what fun he must have had shopping for the accessories listed during the next weeks: a rubber mat, auto robe, vase-and-flower, auto fringe (whatever that was), chamois, and a new suit, shirt, and tie.

His final expense in May:

Auto license	$3.00
Auto insurance	$24.00

And then his troubles began.

June

Repair garage door	$5.00
Auto repairs	$6.00
Auto sill	.50
Carfare (4 @ 5 Cents)	.20

During July "gas and oil--$1.20" appeared four times, indicating increased activity. But more problems soon arose.

July

Repair	$8.50
Black auto paint	.75
Auto from ditch	$5.00
New wheels (2)	$16.00
Carfare (5 @ 5 cents)	.25
Tow line	$1.00
Chicago Auto Club	$11.00

The last item probably resulted from pressure applied by my father. But it didn't stem the flood of minor annoyance during August.

Repair neighbor's garage door	$12.50
Auto repair	$20.00
Black auto paint	.75
Tire and tube	$15.00
Wheel rim	$2.00

Toward the end of August came a flurry of shopping. Grandpa planned a break from the aggravations of his rooming house.

Auto running board box	$3.15
Auto gas stove	$6.00
Fry pan for auto	$1.18
Pocket map	$1.00
Fishing pole	$1.75

September began with four days bracketed together, probably the Labor Day weekend, and for Grandpa, apparently, a very specific weekend.

Aug. 30

Gas and oil	$1.20
Food	$1.45
Fox Lake camp ground	
(3 nights @ 50 cents)	$1.50

Aug. 31

Dance (2 @ 75 cents)	$1.50
Ice cream sodas (2 @ 25 cents)	.50

Sept. 1

Rowboat	$1.25
Corsage	.75
Dinner (2 @ $1.50 and tip)	$3.25
Dance (2 @ 75 cents)	$1.50

Sept. 2

Breakfast (2 @ 65 cents)	$1.30
Souvenir bracelet	$1.32
Souvenir ashtray	.73
Gas and oil to Chicago	$1.15

Home once again, Grandpa fell back into his old routine.

Repair neighbor's steps	$22.50
Auto repairs	$13.00
New clutch	$5.25
Carfare (7 @ 5 cents)	.35

October

Repair garage door	$5.00
Auto repairs	$3.00
Headlights	$1.82
Auto insurance	$35.00

November

Repair brick wall	$15.00
Black auto paint	.75
New gas cap	.65
Auto battery	$13.60

In December, misfortunes followed one another like a series of blizzards:

Repair garage door	$5.00
Repair brake	$5.35
Black auto paint	.75

Tear down busted brick wall	$5.00
Auto fender	$5.50
New rear axle	$13.55
Doctor	$2.00
Arnica and iodine	.45
Dentist pull 2 teeth	$2.00

The old man's feisty spirit collapsed. Two pitiful entries brought the glorious adventure to an abrupt close:

Auto for sale sign	$2.65
Garage for rent sign	.20

I recalled Mother saying that Christmas: "Grandpa phoned from the Aurora Elgin station. I do hope he wore his rubbers so he won't slip on the ice." And Dad sighed, "Thank goodness he's on foot again. A 70-year-old man has no business driving a car."

My eyes returned to the yellowed photo. Dear, spunky, little close-mouthed Grandpa. Did the lady at Fox Lake blush with pleasure over that 75-cent corsage? Did she smile coquettishly from her seat in the rowboat, trailing her hand in the water like the Gibson Girls? Did she vow to think of you whenever she wore the bracelet?

Now I know why you scolded when I broke the ugly Fox Lake ashtray and why we found it, years later, carefully mended and hidden among your handkerchiefs.

Did that three-day romance compensate for all the sadness of your being too old to drive? I'd like to think so.

(Margaret H. Loupy)

Through developing lists of events of emotional intensity, we now have a characterization that we can set in action and the basic outline of a plot. From the lists that we have developed from the data of the ledger, we also have a rough idea of how the plot will unfold, and we have sufficient details to develop the individual scenes. The next step is to build the scenes of the plot.

Building the Scenes of a Plot. One reccuring question in a basic exposition course is when and where to end a paragraph and begin a new one. Most beginning writers have little idea as to what constitutes a paragraph much less when to begin and end one. The same problem comes up almost immediately in a creative writing course but in a different form: when and where does the new scene begin? In fact, the paragraph in an exposition functions in a very similar way to the scene in the narrative. Both are major conceptual or intellectual divisions that by their very construction advance the thesis or, in creative writing, the basic theme and conflict of the narrative.

We have already considered the theme or premise of the narrative. It is much like the thesis of the expository paper. In an expository paper, the thesis is the basic concept that the writer is establishing or proving. In the example of exposition earlier, the writer's thesis was that Grandma Redman was a "courageous, indomitable little lady." The writer proceeded to show that unconquerable courage in three supporting ideas: she clung to the land and her home, she kept the farm functioning, and she overcame the nagging problem of money. The paper is not as strong as it could be because of the overlap in the last two ideas: one of the problems of keeping the farm running was the nagging problem of money. Still, the author provided detailed examples that backed up and established all these ideas. In writing the paper, each of these three ideas with the supporting details would logically become a separate paragraph; thus the progression from one idea to the next idea would signal the ending and beginning of a paragraph. If the main idea of the supporting paragraphs required multiple supporting details, as is the case in this paper, then the writer would have to consider multiple paragraphs for each of the main points he is making. In this case, a reasonable logic for ending and beginning paragraphs might well be the use of different kinds of examples.

Much the same idea holds for the narrative. Russell Baker's book *Growing Up* makes a good case in point. Baker's story is a series of incidents that do not occur randomly but build to a logical climax. In considering Baker's *Growing Up*, I referred earlier to his theme of sexual maturation, in other words the struggle of his growing sexual awareness first against his natural doubts about himself as a man and later clearly against his mother's determination to remain the dominant female in his life (man against himself, and man against man or woman). There are other themes in the book, but this is certainly one of the most obvious and arresting ones. The basic premise might be articulated as Baker's sexual maturation, which was a slow and agonizing process, in which he gradually established his own masculine independence. If this is the basic theme of the narrative, then each major idea must in some way contribute to that theme. He first notices one of his friend's successes with women, then listens to his Uncle Jack fumble through a lecture on the "birds and the bees," then narrowly escapes a sordid brush with a very questionable older man, then fumbles through encounter after encounter with confused and confusing women, and finally meets Mimi. Each idea continues the conflict between two aspects of his personality until the point when he must introduce Mimi to his mother, the first and most formidable female in his life. This final idea, the meeting and relationship of Mimi and his mother, brings the basic theme of the narrative to a conclusion with the confrontation of son with mother (man against man or woman). Now each of these ideas, a building block or expansion of the basic conflict of the narrative, builds in an ascending order of emotional intensity. When Baker establishes his own independence and thus achieves full sexual maturity, the conflict is resolved;

and essentially the narrative--at least this aspect of the narrative--is over. Each step in this conflict, then, is a scene. When the writer has sufficiently explored and expanded what he feels he must about the particular scene, he then ends the scene and begins another.

There is another and perhaps simpler way to approach the problem: the "French scene," a concept used in drama. The French scene is essentially the introduction or exit of an important character. If we return to the Baker example, we see immediately how each scene involves a new, important character: Baker's young friend; Uncle Jack; the sordid older man; the confused and confusing women; Mimi; and finally Mimi and his mother.

Whichever mode of analysis, the author has obviously ignored character encounters or material that does not bear on the theme to emphasize those encounters or items of emotional intensity, those significant encounters that bear directly on the basic conflict of the plot. There is nothing wrong with that; in telling a story we all ignore what we consider to be trivia or unimportant events as we "make the point." If the author feels strongly about preserving all the details at his disposal, he could even place items or character encounters that do not bear on the central purpose of the narrative in a genealogical footnote at the back of the narrative. Or they may give rise to another theme, another plot, and another story. But by sketching out first the basic theme or premise of the narrative, then the increments or specific scenes of the basic conflict, and finally the culminating scene of the narrative where the writer resolves the basic conflict, we have actually written a plot outline. The details of the narrative need now only follow.

Now for some general rules about writing each individual scene. As with any piece of writing, the first rule is to say something that will attract and hold the interest of the reader. This can be a statement, a description, or a dialogue--anything that will arrest the reader's attention. The same advice holds for writers of the basic expository paper: the opening statement of the theme as well as the opening statement of the each support paragraph should begin with something that will make the reader want to continue reading. With the narrative, there are as many kinds of openings as there are types of prose and kinds of writers. Russell Baker in *Growing Up*, begins a chapter--a scene--about his father with the following: "During all these years my father was under a sentence of death." Ben Ames Williams, in a scene in *Come Spring* that deals with a disastrous storm, begins with "Winter laid so firm a grasp upon them that it seemed a permanent condition, like a wakeful night when the hours are endless till the reluctant dawn." Both of these openings are examples of how the writer of the narrative can arrest the attention of the reader.

The second rule is that each scene must advance the basic conflict of the theme or premise of the narrative in a block that is a complete unit to itself. In fact, that is the definition of a scene: a division in which the action is continuous, and there is no shift of place and time. Wallace

Stegner, in *Angle of Repose*, captures the reader's interest with the opening line: "Today was Rodman day. He might as well have put a gun to my head." It is obvious that the basic conflict of this scene is between Rodman and his father. Then for several pages, Stegner presents the scene in which Rodman and his father are at odds over the story that the father is writing. There are many purposes to the scene: Rodman's need to bring his estranged father and mother together, which also pits the son and the father against one another; the basic husband-wife conflict of the book that the father is writing, which is an exposition of a failed marital relationship; and the father's consuming interest in the basic problem of the narrative, which pits the father's need to understand exactly what happened to his ancestors with his own inadequate physical stamina. Whatever the conflict or conflicts, the scene is complete when the author has achieved what he wants to achieve in elaborating on the conflict between Rodman and his father. Ben Ames Williams is not the writer that Stegner is with his complex, interacting scenes, but he does essentially the same thing. The winter scene referred to in the above paragraph deals with a terrible storm that isolates the family, and a mother who gives birth to a dead baby. Williams's next scene begins with early March. The winter scene is complete because there has been no shift in place and time, and the conflict within the scene is continuous up to the end of the scene.

The third rule is that the final scene, as in the final paragraph of a theme, must conclude in some way the basic conflict of the story. That does not mean that the conflict has to be resolved. If it is, we term it a closed plot; if it is not, we term it an open plot. The final scene brings together all the various parts of that theme in an ending that concludes, explains, clarifies, or resolves the basic problem of the theme. And the final scene, as in the concluding paragraph of an expository paper, must end with some kind of a send-off, a statement or idea expressed in some way that is new or different from the theme yet grows out of that basic theme. Stegner in his final scene concludes the theme of the narrative explaining and clarifying the basic problem of the narrative. The husband came back to live with his wife in a permanent "angle of repose," living together but never forgiving and overlooking the mistakes of the past: "In all the years I lived with them I never saw them kiss, I never saw them put their arms around each other, I never saw them touch!" And then the send-off, the revelation or insight that grows out of the narrative, explaining the narrator's personal inability to mend the broken fences of his own marriage, and touches us all with its basic and prophetic humanity: "In this not-quite-quiet darkness, while the Diesel breaks its heart more and more faintly on the mountain grade, I lie wondering if I am man enough to be a bigger man than my grandfather." Easy to describe, but not so easy to do.

Let me illustrate the problems and the process with a student paper. This paper was not intended as a narrative but more as a chronicle--a chronological listing about a man's life; but since many writers of the family narrative find it easier first to arrange in chronological order the details of a man's life and later to move on to a more complete narrative, this student's paper makes a good starting point. The process works well in this case because in many ways the chronicle below is the plot outline of what could be a much longer and more detailed narrative. The student divided the story more or less into seven segments, some of which are already clearly scenes: the first relating his chance discovery of the grave marker when he was a child; the second a transition in which the author describes his development as a family historian or genealogist and the events surrounding the discovery of important letters; the third in which he deals with events in Virginia, including the purchase of Aunt Hannah's husband; the fourth in which he discusses the family's life in Missouri; the fifth in which he describes the loss and shock of the Civil War; the sixth in which he presents the protagonist's tragic and almost trivial death; and the final in which he returns to a discussion of his own feelings. Consider whether each scene advances a theme or basic conflict and whether the story builds to an inevitable resolution, or whether the paper simply presents the chronological details of a man's life as the writer researched and isolated them.

A Man Called Henry Millan

[Segment One: Discovery of the Grave Marker]

On a tree-shaded hill on the edge of a little Iowa town lies a small cemetery. It has served as the final resting place of the local citizens since the founding of the town, more than one hundred and fifty years ago. Summer breezes play through the trees, causing the leaves to respond with gentle sighs and whispers. In the winter, snow clings to the bare branches, and the graves are covered with a mantle of crystalline white.

Halfway down the hillside stands a small marble obelisk. Its once white, polished surface is gray and grainy, the victim of countless rains and snows. In the shifting shadows, colonies of lichen grow, slowly eating their way across names chiseled on the marble almost a hundred years ago. Careful brushing and close examination reveal the image of a crown. Beneath it, in old-fashioned letters, is the inscription:

Henry S. Millan
Born Nov. 14, 1802
Died Aug. 19, 1888

I first made the chance discovery of the obelisk long ago when I was still a child. The name on the stone caught my attention. Millan was my Grandfather Hooper's middle name and his mother's maiden name. Might I be related to Henry Millan? Could he be an ancestor of mine? Childlike, I soon lost interest. I had too much to learn about the living world and my place in it to think much about dead forebears.

[Segment Two: Development as a Family Historian]

It was only years later, after I retired and took up genealogy as a hobby, that I had the time to pursue the mystery of Henry Millan's identity. Research brought to light bits and pieces of his life. Census records gave names and dates. Wills told of prized possessions. Court and military records added more names and events. Slowly the statistical form of Henry Millan emerged; but the human substance of the man was still missing.

Then a series of events occurred that made it possible to see Henry as he appeared to his family and friends. An aunt, in going through my recently deceased Grandmother's papers, found some brittle yellow newspapers containing family obituaries. A woman researching a book on the history of Lucas County, Iowa, located a journal written by Henry's daughter, Susanna Millan Custer. And last year a man became intrigued by a bundle of letters he saw lying on a nearby trash heap.

[Segment Three: Events in Virginia]

Susanna's journal makes the image of the young Henry Millan come to life. "Tall, dark and handsome" is Susanna's description of her father. A stalwart and progressive man who was awarded a captaincy in the Virginia State Militia, he was fiercely proud of his family's connections with the landed aristocracy of Virginia. He took an active part in politics and worked hard for the election to the presidency of his friends and fellow Virginians John Tyler and William H. Harrison.

When Henry married the young Caroline Farr, he purchased a deserted, vine-clad stone house that had been the property of Tories who had fled Virginia during the Revolutionary War. He was partial to the permanency of a stone house and liked the ancient trees and spacious lawns surrounding this one. Using the help of his slaves, he proceeded to renovate the house and furnish it for the large family that he hoped to have. Soon, however, his young bride became unhappy with the lonely isolation of her home in the country. At night the moaning of the wind and the scurrying of little feet in the attic disturbed her. Her slaves insisted that the sounds were those of the ghosts of the "Britishers" who were lying in wait for their mistress, planning to carry her off.

The Captain was disgusted with the "ghost" talk, but when he realized how unhappy his wife was, he reluctantly gave up his beloved stone house and purchased a frame one from a relative who was migrating West. The new home had formal gardens, arbors, lawn seats and a family cemetery surrounded by pear and peach trees.

Within a few years the yields from the tobacco fields started declining, and the Captain became restless. His elder brother, who had emigrated West a few years earlier, kept sending Henry letters urging him to come to Missouri where fertile land could be purchased cheaply. Finally, in spite of the protest of the Millan and Farr families, Henry decided to sell his holdings in Virginia and join his brother in Missouri.

One of the problems facing Henry was the disposal of his slaves. Most of the field and house slaves were sold to relatives. A few were to receive their freedom. One slave who refused to be either sold or freed was the children's nurse Aunt Hannah. She had been Caroline's childhood nurse and had become a member of the Millan household upon Caroline's marriage to Henry. With her insistence upon remaining with "her family" a problem arose, because Aunt Hannah's husband Ben belonged to another family. Susanna describes the departure scene for us.

"Everyone was weeping, caught in the agony of farewells, and not the least was dear old black Aunt Hannah, in whose spacious and generous arms each Millan child had been tenderly nursed. Aunt Hannah refused to be left behind. She could not part from her mistress' family, nor could she bear to leave her husband Uncle Ben, who was owned by another planter. When he came over to bid her goodbye, fruitful rivers in the eyes of all were loosened in a flood of tears, and shattering sobs took hold of everyone. It was too much for my father. He mounted his horse, rode over and bought Uncle Ben for $800. Returning, he told Uncle Ben to go get his clothes and come along. Uncle Ben threw his hat on the ground, gave Mrs. Millan a tremendous hug and turned to the Captain crying. "God will bless you for this, Marse Henry."

This event, according to Susanna, had a profound effect upon Henry. "It was here that my father first realized that his compassion was stronger than his business instincts," she wrote. It was probably at this time that the young Virginia slave owner first began to be aware of the evils inherent in the institution of slavery.

[Segment Four: Life in Missouri]

The family and its possessions were loaded into a huge schooner-type of wagon that required a team of six horses to pull it. After eight days of travel, they reached the Ohio River. There the family, with its personal belongings, boarded a steamer that carried it to a junction with the Mississippi River, then northward to Green's Landing twelve miles north of Hannibal. Uncle Ben was left behind to bring the household possessions overland in the wagon. So great was Henry's confidence in Ben that he directed him to travel the shorter route that would take him through the free states north of the Ohio River where technically Ben was a free man.

Henry prospered with his new lands near Canton, Missouri. He was pleased with the "common schools" which he felt were superior to those of Virginia. After graduation, each child was sent to a private academy. He insisted that his daughters, as well as his sons, have at least five years of classical education in which they learned English and American history, Latin, higher mathematics and astronomy.

After a few years, the family moved to the small town of Lancaster where they became acquainted with another family from Virginia, the Custers. "They had three daughters and one shy, bashful son who was greatly attracted to Miss Susanna, but her father had laid down the law that any man she wished to marry must be a Virginian, a Whig, and a Methodist. The Custer family scored on the first qualification but "alas and alack" they were Democrats and Presbyterians! But love finds a way. The unacceptable was changed to the acceptable and wedding bells rang, not only for James B. Custer and Susanna Millan, but for two other young people in these families."

Susanna and her new husband purchased a farm in the newly opened lands of Lucas County, Iowa. James had been commissioned by the government to help survey the area a year earlier, and he had been impressed with the richness of the prairie soil. He and Susanna tried to get Henry to join them in their move northward, but he refused, saying that he had no desire to live in a free state.

At this point, Susanna's journal ceases to be a good source of material on Henry's life. She left her Missouri home to start a family of her own, and her journal no longer dealt with a daughter's relationship to her parents, but rather with that of a wife to her husband. Fortunately the letters rescued from the city dump give us a glimpse of Henry in his later years.

[Segment Five: The Loss and Shock of the Civil War]

For fourteen years after Susanna's wedding, Henry and Caroline and the younger children remained in Missouri; but in 1861, northern Missouri exploded into full-scale civil war. Groups of southern sympathizers organized themselves into a state militia to support the pro-secessionist Missouri governor. The pro-Union group responded by organizing the Rome Guards to oppose any attempt on the part of the governor to take Missouri out of the Union.

Each of these units roamed the countryside preying upon the other. At various times, the towns of Kirksville, Lancaster, and Palmyra were seized by one group and then besieged by the other. Henry, fearing for the safety of his family, moved them northward to join Susanna and her husband in Chariton, Iowa. Henry was, at this time, fifty-nine years old.

The family was barely settled when the twenty-four-year-old son Stanton joined Company K, Third Iowa Volunteer Cavalry to fight for the Union. On January 31, 1862, he was stationed in Missouri where he wrote his father that he expected that his unit would "be kept in Missouri." Four months later, on May 30, 1862, Stanton was killed in a minor skirmish on a lonely hill in Arkansas. Within two years the family suffered another loss in the death of fifteen-year-old Lavinia, youngest of the Millan children. Henry and his wife were devastated by these losses.

During the war, communication between Henry and his Virginia relatives had not been possible, but at war's end he wrote to a favorite sister Jane S. Johnson about his grief. She promptly replied with a letter dated December 30, 1867, Fairfax County, Virginia:

I sincerely sympathize with you and Sister Caroline in the loss of your dear children. I know from experience what it is to lose a dearly beloved child. I lost my oldest Tom some years ago, and during the war one of my twins Frank who was fighting with the Army of Virginia was taken prisoner by the Union Army.

When captured he was badly wounded and quite ill. When I learned that he was dying, I tried to go to him, but I was refused a pass through Union lines. My son was a brave officer and died in defense of his country. He was truly lamented by his company as well as all of his friends, but oh, my dear brother, it was the greatest trial that I ever had to bear with. Not that I have not lost others as dear to me as he was but I had them with me and I did all I could for them, but him I could not go see. After his death I received several letters from northern ladies who were permitted to visit him during his sickness. They told me that I might rest assured that everything that could be done was done for his comfort. They went every day and carried him every nourishment that was needful. They said that he had one of the best of doctors and was very kind to him. My dear brother, the Lord gives us children and He takes them away to be with Him. Blessed be His name. It is our duty to be resigned to His will. But oh! It is so hard to give him up. I feel as if I shall never get over his death.

The last time I ever saw him he was looking so pert and hearty and was in such fine spirits. I would send you his obituary but I have but one. It gives him a grateful name as a brave officer. My dear brother, I do so feel for the loss of your sweet young daughter and your brave soldier son. I'm so sorry that his body was never recovered from the battlefield to be sent to you for proper Christian burial.

The letter then continues, describing to Henry the destruction that had occurred in northern Virginia because of the war and the attempts of their various relatives to rebuild their shattered lives.

[Segment Six: Death of the Protagonist]

A final bit of information on Henry's life comes from two yellowed family obituaries, carefully clipped from the Orleans, Nebraska, newspaper by his daughter Pocahantas Millan Hooper. Both are dated 1888, some twenty-one years after the above letter. The first one relates the death of Caroline. On February 3, 1888, Henry's wife and beloved companion of over sixty years died after a brief illness. For six months Henry struggled to cope with his loss. This proud man who for years had been a tower of strength for his family was now a lonely, infirm old man who dreaded becoming a burden on his family. The following obituary completes the story of Henry's life:

On Sunday afternoon Mrs. M. G. Hooper received the news by telephone of the death of her aged father, in Chariton, Iowa. About two weeks previous, Mr. Millan was walking upon the railroad track when a slow moving train struck him, landing him upon the pilot of the engine. The engineer saw him on the track but did not whistle or ring the bell, thinking he would get off before reaching him, and did not see him when he was struck, but carried him about a mile, when he was thrown off or crawled off. Upon his being examined his head was found badly bruised up and his collar bone broken. Mr. Millan never fully recovered consciousness and died last Sunday afternoon at four o'clock. He was past 86 years old.

[Segment Seven: The Author Discusses His Own Feelings]

Last year I visited the Chariton cemetery and made my way to the ancient, eroding obelisk with the name of my great, great-grandfather carved on it. A kaleidoscope of images raced through my mind. The darkly handsome Captain, so confidently planning a home for his bride-to-be. The young husband dreaming of a new life on the western frontier. The slave owner discovering that compassion for a fellow human being is more important than monetary gain. The middle-aged man experiencing the horrors of a civil war that placed him and his brother and sisters on opposing sides. The bewildered father grieving over the death of two children. The frail old man suffering the aching loneliness of the loss of his lifetime companion.

I feel a close kindredship with this man who lived so long ago, in a world so different from mine, for we share more than just family ties. We share a common humanity.

(Harry Hooper)

The story about Henry Millan concludes with a final and dismal death. It is poignant largely because Henry at one time commanded a very formidable reputation, and to see such a man die so ignominiously on a "cow catcher" strikes us all as tragic and unnecessary. But because this is a story-chronicle, the purpose of which is simply to establish the basic chronology of the man's life, Henry's death is not the inevitable conclusion or resolution of a conflict. In the author's words, "a series of events occurred that made it possible to see Henry as he appeared to his family and friends." His daughter sees him as a practical businessman who seems almost surprised with himself when he discovers that his compassion is stronger than his business sense. We have no idea what he wrote his sister in Virginia at the close of the war although his sister's letter reveals that he must have suffered greatly. The author then characterizes Henry as a "lonely, infirm old man who dreaded becoming a burden on his family" and completes the portrait with Henry's death on a "cow catcher." The portrait is sensitive and moving, and we all agree that the author has established Millan's "human substance." But the piece does not involve a basic conflict, and the ending does not conclude a basic conflict. Life is hard, but there is nothing in Henry's life that brought him inevitably to this conclusion. The author faintly suggests that Henry may have taken his own life to save his family any burden which further establishes Henry's basic "human substance." But if we interpret the circumstances of his death as an accident, the death is senseless, so completely unwarranted and unsuspected. Henry's earlier life of adaptation and sensitivity ends with a terrible and senseless death, and this contrast leaves us stunned. Life simply rolls on, senselessly taking up the proud with the poor and humble in its cow catcher of agony. The story is moving, the author's purpose is achieved, but there is no basic conflict which each scene builds on until the final scene when that conflict is concluded. Before we take the steps to introduce a conflict into this story-chronicle or to rewrite this chronicle as a narrative, let us first turn our attention to coherence, an important ingredient in tying together the various parts or segments of a story.

Coherence: Binding the Story Together. It may seem inappropriate to suddenly shift our attention from subjects like characterization and plot to coherence, but coherence, or more correctly the lack of coherence, is a problem that comes up constantly with a beginning writer of the family narrative. Probably because the beginning writer of the family narrative is normally a genealogist who has pulled ideas and facts from here and there, he often produces a narrative that is as disjointed as the details from his files, pedigree charts, and family group sheets. The following is taken from a student paper filled with details that all relate to the story; however, the author has not arranged the various parts of the composition so as to make the movement from sentence to sentence or paragraph to paragraph clear and logical (in other words, coherent). The resulting account is confusing. To make analysis easier, I have numbered the various paragraphs of this story.

(1) General Davis with approximately 20,000 northern troops marched on Rome, Georgia. The artillery was able to hold them off for a day, but the small garrison of five thousand soldiers under General Stuart was no match for the superiority of the northern army. To avoid the heavy cannonading, the Confederate troops were ordered on May 17, 1864, to evacuate. They pulled out that night rummaging stores.

(2) About 11 o'clock the next day, the enemy occupied Rome. Several buildings were torn down so that the lumber could be used to build huts. The land lay desolate. All the edible food had been stripped from the fields. Much of the ground was covered with growth. Plows could be seen in the fields, abandoned by the farmers who had answered the call. Almost every boy and man between the ages of 15 and 60 had joined the army.

(3) Out in the country, near the foot of Horseleg Mountain, there lived a little boy named Billy. He was only eight years old when the Yankee soldiers invaded the countryside.

(4) When Billy saw some Yankee soldiers going into the bar, he hid in the fireplace, for he knew that if the soldiers saw him, they would have forced him to tell where the bull had been hid. The bull was all the local women had to carry grain to the mill and to perform other heavy tasks.

(5) That evening, the captain came to see his girlfriend. She would not have anything to do with him, of course. It was her friends that were going to suffer hardship without the help of the bull. The following day, the captain found out why she would not speak to him. He then gave the order to his men who were planning to barbecue the poor old beast to release him. A tag was placed in the bull's ear guaranteeing his freedom. The bull had been spared, but Rome's fate was still in the hands of her captors.

The first problem occurs with the second sentence of paragraph (1). We know that Davis and his northern troops are marching on Rome, but we are not exactly clear as to whose artillery is holding "them off for a day," particularly when we read that the Confederate troops evacuated the town "to avoid heavy cannonading." There is also some confusion as to the sequence of events in the last sentence. Obviously, the troops pulled out after rummaging the stores, an idea that is important to understanding the plight of the occupying army. We need to change "rummaging" to "having rummaged" to show the exact relationship in time between the two events that the last sentence describes. Now consider paragraphs (2) and (3).

Here we are confused with a puzzling jump. The author indicates in paragraph (3) that the scene shifts from the town to "the country" or as he later in paragraph (3) terms it "the countryside." But what is the relationship between the "land" and the town in paragraph (2)? We have been reading about the invasion of the town of Rome, not the invasion of the countryside. It would be helpful to add the phrase "and the surrounding region" to the first sentence of paragraph (2): "About 11 o'clock the next day, the enemy occupied Rome and the surrounding region." Then we would know that the invasion has included an area broader than that of the town of Rome and that "the land" is in contrast to the town of Rome. We are now prepared for the events near Horseleg Mountain. The story now continues with paragraph (4).

We are clear as to the introduction of Billy, but we know nothing about "the barn." Whose barn is it: a neighbor's, or his family's? Why exactly are the soldiers spending their time looking for a bull when there is a war to be fought? Did they find Billy in the fireplace? Are we to assume that the bull is hid in the barn or that the soldiers were looking in the wrong place and that Billy was forced to reveal the hiding place of the bull? And what does the bull have to do with the story? There is also such a big jump between paragraphs (3) and (4) that we need more than a word or phrase to tie these two paragraphs together. We need a transition paragraph although a statement as to the soldiers' motive in hunting down the bull should appear earlier, probably in paragraph (2). In order to enhance the flow from the third to the fourth paragraphs, we need some help in understanding the change of time. The word "when" is simply too ambiguous. The phrase "one day shortly after the invasion of the northern troops" would probably work as well as any.

In considering paragraph (5), we are again confused. Who is the captain? We would probably assume that he is someone attached to the invading army, but we really do not know. What is the relationship between the "girlfriend" and the women in the preceding paragraph? Is she one of them, or is she someone from the captain's hometown who has some sympathy for the plight of the local women? Also the author has failed to inform us of a very significant detail in the story: that the northern troops have apparently found the bull and that the local women have in some way influenced the captain's girlfriend to help them regain the bull for the use of the local populace.

Assuming these changes, consider these five paragraphs again. The changes are italicized:

(1) General Davis with approximately 20,000 northern troops

marched on Rome, Georgia. The *southern* artillery was able to hold them off for a day, but the small garrison of five thousand soldiers under General Stuart was no match for the superiority of the northern army. To avoid the heavy cannonading, General Stuart ordered his troops to evacuate Rome on May 17, 1864. They pulled out that night *having rummaged* the stores.

(2) About 11 o'clock the next day, the enemy occupied Rome and *the surrounding region.* They tore down several buildings so that they could use the lumber to build huts for shelter; *but their supplies were so meager that they were forced along with the local populace to forage the countryside for food.* The land, *however,* lay desolate. Starving people had already stripped all the edible food from the fields, and growth covered much of the land. Plows lay in the fields, abandoned by the farmers who had answered the call. Almost every boy and man between the ages of 15 and 60 had joined the army.

(3) In the countryside near the foot of Horseleg Mountain, a little eight-year-old boy lived *alone with his mother. They along with everyone else were trying to live off the land.* Billy's mother had managed to keep one old bull alive which the local women used to carry grain to the mill and to perform other heavy tasks. To keep the bull from being discovered and eaten by the hungry northern soldiers, Billy's mother kept the bull hidden inside their barn. And she had cautioned Billy that he was to reveal the location of the animal to no one.

(4) *Shortly after the northern troops had occupied the region, Billy noticed some Yankee soldiers stop in front of their property.* He hid in the fireplace because he knew that if the soldiers saw him, they would force him to tell where his mother had hid the bull. The bull would have made an excellent meal to the hungry soldiers. Billy's caution was of no avail, however, for he soon heard the soldiers leading the animal away.

(5) That evening, the captain of the soldiers who had taken the bull came to visit his girlfriend, *a local woman who along with the other women in the area depended on the bull.* She refused to have anything to do with the northern captain. *Confused, the captain returned to his camp;* the following day, the captain found out why she would not speak to him. *He learned that it was the friends of his girlfriend who were going to suffer without the help of the bull.* He then gave the order to his men who were planning to barbecue the poor old beast to release him. They placed a tag in the bull's ear guaranteeing his freedom. The bull had survived, but Rome's fate was still in the hands of her captors.

This process of gluing the sentences and the paragraphs into a smooth, readable whole is known as providing coherence. There are several ways of building coherence into a paragraph or a narrative. The most common kind of device that the author can use to build coherence is to repeat key words or phrases. We clarified the distinction between the town of Rome and the countryside by repeating or adding key words or phrases that helped bind the story together: "the surrounding region," "countryside," and we added "hungry" to the word captors. An other important way to achieve coherence is to set segments of the story firmly in time or space; when we give a segment of the story an exact time or an exact place, we can relate other segments or sections to it because we now know that they occurred before or after: "having rummaged" and "shortly after" (more exact than when). Another method is to use transitional words that show the relationship between sentences or ideas: "but," "along with," and "however." Other examples of transitional words are "also," "besides," "further," "in addition," "moreover," and "too," which signal addition; "yet," "in contrast," "nevertheless," "on the contrary," and "on the other hand," which signal contrast; "as a result," "consequently," "hence," "therefore," and "thus," which signal cause and effect; "in conclusion," "to conclude," and "to summarize," which signal summary; and "likewise" and "similarly," which signal comparison. Of course, we have added entire sentences and paragraphs that bridge the sudden jumps in the original five-paragraph story. Many beginning writers make the assumption that the reader follows every turn and shift they make. After all, the story is clear to them, why not to everyone else. The fact is that no reader can follow an author who does not leave clear signposts along the way. Now that we have established the importance of linking elements in a narrative with clear mental signals, let us return to the earlier discussion of plot development.

PLOT CONFLICT

One question that students continually raise is what about those stories that have no plot or those stories in which plot plays a very minor role. Actually, plotless stories are not as common as one might think, and the fact remains that most readers would find a story without a plot unappealing; still this kind of a story is a reasonable alternative, particularly for the family historian who is more interested in leaving a good record than a moving narrative. E. M. Forster made a very useful distinction between what he called a "story" and a plot: a "story" is a "narrative of events in their time sequence. A plot is also a narrative of events, the emphasis falling on causality" (see C. Hugh Holman et al., *A Handbook to Literature*). By selecting and arranging incidents, the writer of the plot builds through a major conflict/focus to an inevitable conclusion. The plot is, simply put, a series of actions working for or against the central character. The "story," to use Forster's terminology, simply records events as they occur with no attempt to build to an inevitable climax or resolution. Perhaps the best way to see the distinction between a narrative with a conflict/theme or basic premise and a story-chronicle (having a chronological rather than causal ordering of events) that simply records the events of a life is to turn to Willa Cather who left us several novels that qualify as family chronicles or "stories": *Shadows on the Rock, O Pioneer,* and *My Ántonia.*

Cather's *Shadows on the Rock* deals with the French in Quebec, specifically with Euclide Auclair, an apothecary of Quebec, and his daughter Cecile. The novel is divided into six sections: "The Apothecary," "Cecile and Jacques," "The Long Winter," "Pierre Charron," "The Ships from France," and "The Dying Count." Each of the six sections is really a separate and unrelated incident connected only because each deals with the same set of lives. In the final section, "The Dying Count," the daughter Cecile is reported to have married Pierre Charron, the subject of the fourth section, but Cecil otherwise drops from the story even though the first five sections of the novel have dealt almost exclusively with her. The death of the count means that the old apothecary and his daughter Cecile will never return to France, a return that Cecile has actually long wanted to avoid making. Almost as an afterthought, there is the epilogue. The bishop returns after some thirteen years from France, broken and old but in some ways spiritually matured in his imposed humility. The apothecary, however, has not felt the effects of time and has in fact changed very little. The bishop and the apothecary talk about the King's loss in the death of his grandson, the King's declining spirits, and the marriage of the apothecary's daughter Cecile, and her four sons. And then the final paragraph of the story:

> While he was closing his shop and changing his coat to go up to his daughter's house, he thought over much that his visitor had told him, and he believed that he was indeed fortunate to spend his old age here where nothing changed; to watch his grandsons grow up in a country where the death of the King, the probable evils of a long regency, would never touch them.
>
> (Willa Cather, *Shadows on the Rock*)

End of story! The descriptions are tender and sensitive. The characters warm and winning. The decline and demise of the haughty bishop and determined count are contrasted with the apothecary's quiet, personal strength, a contrast that moves us. But nowhere is there a theme with a conflict or series of conflicts building to a final resolution. The bishop and the count were enemies when both were young, but one dies while the other is in France; and the other grows old and humble. The wilderness is always there breaking and destroying men, but it is very definitely in the background. Life simply goes on in its inevitable cycle. Nowhere is there a basic conflict that ties the story together and resolves itself at the end. Instead there is simply the peaceful, almost quiet, descriptions of character and scene ending with the main character in the story simply closing his shop.

Even narratives with plots, though, can give the impression of plotlessness by muting the plot through techniques such as flashback. One simply rearranges the time segments so that the flow of time is altered or changed so much that the reader fails to see the theme conflict or premise of the narrative as easily as he would if events were arranged chronologically. There are many ways to rearrange the segments of a story chronologically. Flashback is a device that we all use in conversation. We tell a story, stopping suddenly to fill in the listener with more background information or moving quickly to a parallel story. We all know how distracting, though, this technique can be particularly with a mind that would rather jump all over the mental map rather than finish telling the story. The story-chronicle about Henry Millan, which has no real plot, employs a kind of flashback technique. First of all, the story begins with the author's awakening interest in his family's past. It starts with some chance encounters in his youth, and it develops with his growing interest in genealogy and the recovery of a critical journal. We know that something significant for the author is about to happen, something that has been waiting quietly in the corners of his mind. Then the story of Henry Millan is told. And at the end of the story, we return to the author who speaks of his "common humanity" with an ancestor who "lived so long ago." Within this frame, the author tells the story about Henry Millan. In other words, he stops telling his story about himself to get on with the real purpose of the story, Henry Millan. He could well have begun the story with Henry's daughter's journal, moving chronologically toward Henry's death. But he chose to link his personal story with that of Henry's, and what makes this flashback work so well is that both stories, the author's and Henry's, hang together. Each is related to the other because establishing the human substance of Henry Millan is a personal quest for the author. In other words, there must be some kind of integral relationship between the flashback and the story itself. Otherwise, the reader is jarred and confused by a flashback that is off the subject.

While a well-constructed plot is the hallmark of a good narrative, there is no reason why an author cannot write a simple chronicle or story that moves chronologically from beginning to end and simply ends because the person's life has ended. In fact, the imposition of a plot on a person's life may in many ways be artificial and demand the kind of imaginative filling in of details that the documents do not justify. Literally, the choice is the author's.

Building Conflict into the Plot. We have established that the basic ingredient of the plot is the theme or premise with a conflict. We considered several plot themes--persecution, revenge, overcoming, seizing, solving, familial rivalry, catastrophic circumstances, sacrifice, unequal rivals, love, ambition, mistakes, remorse, and losing--and fitted several plot themes with one or more conflicts. And we stressed the importance of articulating the theme specifically enough so that a workable plot results: e.g., William Grant's need for personal glory brought him criticism from friends and the loss of a valuable contract. The subject is William Grant, and the idea that we are trying to show about William

Grant is that his personal need for glory led ultimately to his loss of a postal contract and public disapproval, essentially a conflict of man versus man. We then discussed the building of scenes, showing how each scene must play out the basic theme or premise of the narrative. But we touched only briefly on the essential element of conflict.

There is no shortage of material on narrative conflict, and normally most agree that there are essentially four kinds of possible conflict: (1) man against nature, which is sometimes divided into man against fate and man against alienation; (2) man against society; (3) man against man; and (4) man against himself or one aspect of a man's personality in conflict with another aspect of the same personality.

If we reduce the story "A Man Called Henry Millan" to an outline that highlights the various conflicts within the story, we are in a better position to understand exactly why the story "A Man Called Henry Millan" is a story-chronicle and does not have a plot:

1. Beginning: setting the scene with the author's interest in family history and introduction of the main characters; the introduction of a minor problem that puts Henry's personal wishes at odds with those of his superstitious wife. The conflict of man versus man (Henry versus his wife) is resolved when Henry reluctantly sells the house.

2. Middle: first major conflict occurs when the family must move from Virginia to Missouri because of declining tobacco yields (man against nature). The next conflict involves Henry's compassion--refusing to allow his business sense to break up a slave family (man against himself). The next conflict pits Henry against one of his children, Susanna, and later against her and her husband when he refuses to move north to a free state (man against man). The next conflict involves Henry's moving north to keep his family out of the battle front in Missouri (man against man). The next conflict pits Henry and his Confederate relatives against nature as they face the common loss of children.

3. End: the final conflict shows Henry's declining health and probably senseless death on an engine's cow catcher (man against nature). Or if we assume that this is a suicide for the purpose of saving his family from the burden of caring for a man failing in health (man against man or himself).

The problem is that the author does not focus on one clear type of conflict. In fact, his story has all four. Now there is no reason why a story cannot have all four conflicts, but there must be a clear conflict focus; one must stand out as the major conflict, particularly in a shorter work such as a short-story narrative. Because there is no clear conflict focus, each scene does not logically lead to the next scene. The resolution of Henry's conflict with his wife's superstitious nature does not lead us to Henry's struggle with nature to maintain his declining tobacco fields nor to his conflict with himself over the sale of a slave. Thus, each scene does not lead to the final culminating scene that would provide the climactic conflict and resolution of the basic conflict stated in the basic theme or premise.

There is another problem to be considered in working conflict into a narrative. It is obvious that too many conflict peaks in a story serve only to wear out the reader. We are all familiar with television dramas that move rapidly from one conflict to another. We are literally worn out by the time the hero has managed to overcome a series of rivals, robberies, rapes, and murders. Some suggest that a rule of thumb is one conflict per 2,000 words. (See Pauline Bloom in her article "Mistreat Your Character," Frank A. Dickson and Sandra Smythe, editors, *The Writer's Digest Handbook of Short Story Writing*, Cincinnati, Ohio: Writer's Digest Books.) In the story-chronicle "A Man Called Henry Millan," there are approximately 2,000 words, room enough for only one conflict, not six or seven.

Assuming that the author wants this story to become a narrative with a plot--we have already discussed the playing down of the plot, a perfectly legitimate alternative--the solution might lie in refocusing the scenes so that they all emphasize one kind of conflict. Let us assume that we want to show Henry's struggle between two aspects of his personality, his concern for others versus his basic human need to preserve his own practical interests. If we then present each scene showing how Henry's compassionate nature overrules his more selfish and egocentric needs, we could give the story a sense of conflict unity that it does not now have. He moves his frightened wife from the best real estate bargain in Virginia; he purchases a slave when he can ill afford it; he allows his children to marry when he would prefer to dictate when and whom they marry; he supports his sister in her hour of need when she represents an enemy who has in effect taken the life of his own son; and finally, he takes his own life when he realizes that his continued existence poses a burden on those whom he loves. Actually, so much of the story already deals with this basic conflict, it would require very little refocusing to bring out this conflict in great strength. What is even more important, though, would be the necessity of going into more detail so that each scene is explored in sufficient detail or of reducing the number of scenes to a manageable one or two. It would take very little refocusing so that each scene would contribute to the final moment in Henry's struggle with himself to put his personal needs second to the needs of the people he loves.

The following student narrative is composed of one scene. Although part of the narrative occurs on Saturday just before noon and part occurs later during the evening of that same day, one could read the narrative as composed of two scenes, but the action and conflict are continuous. We will read it as one scene, built around the basic conflict of the girl versus the grandmother (the man-against-man conflict). The object of the conflict is the teddy bear, which she so desperately wants, which links her with her past, and which the compulsive and ever-clean grandmother does not want her to have. The conflict is resolved in the favor of the small girl when she awakes the next morning; although, we cannot help but suspect that the child will never be allowed to keep the teddy bear. Incidental but crucial to the narrative is the custody con-flict--a secondary conflict--between the grandmother and the so-called "crazy woman": the daughter-in-law and mother of the small girl:

The Happening

An insistent knock sounded at the side door. A few moments before, Betty Jane had watched a brown fur coat coming down the sidewalk towards her house at the end of Kentucky Street. She saw the mottled brown sliding kaleidoscopically between the white pick-ets bordering the front gate, which was always latched. At her eye level, it appeared to be a moving panorama of dark fur, hazy, seem-ingly unpropelled, but deliberately and purposefully approaching the side screen door. For some reason, she remembered the teddy bear she had before her father died when she still lived with her parents somewhere outside the white picket fence. When she showed her grandmother a teddy bear in a store, she was told that teddy bears were silly and that little girls had dolls.

Since she was old enough to know that a fur coat couldn't walk, she said shyly to her grandmother, "That brown fur person is coming to the door again." Grandmother immediately put down her dust cloth--for she was forever dusting and polishing--and spoke sharply, "Come into the bedroom, we must not answer the door. That is a crazy woman out there." An inexplicable wild urge to run to the door stirred in the child. She tried to fathom that feeling--whether it was from curiosity or just a seeking of some action to rebel against the dominating tone of her grandmother or because the "brown fur person" seemed somehow warmly familiar--she could not say. In-deed, at her age, it was just a small trill of a feeling--a wistful yearn-ing--as if invisible ties somehow linked her to that being who made her appearance periodically, for some unknown reason, at their door. Usually it happened on Saturday just before noon and was treated as an insignificant happening in that busy household.

They waited wordlessly as the knocking continued. It seemed like forever to the little girl, and she was almost afraid to breathe, looking up at the stern expression on her grandmother's face. Then there was only silence, and grandmother would say, "I guess she has gone; now I can get back to my cleaning. Go on into the dining room, Betty Jane, and play with your doll." And the little girl would invariably sidle over to a window, trying to get a last glimpse of the strange crazy person moving slowly past the white spikes and the splotches of pink and blue and lavender; and sometimes a face atop the brown would look back towards the window. But strain as she would, peering through the lace curtains, the child could never make out what that face looked like, because it was at least sixty feet across a broad expanse of lawn to the front gate--the little house being located at the extreme rear of a large lot.

Nothing more was said about the Saturday mystery, and household activities continued as before in a sort of empty vacuum, which to the child seemed to match her own expressionless world, punctuated verbally by her Grandmother's words and silently by the little girl's own dark brooding thoughts.

That evening, like so many others, she was carefully tucked into her oversized iron crib with the words, "It's time to go to sleep now," and Betty Jane made no comment, but dutifully closed her eyes. In a little while she drifted off as usual, not to a child's sugarplum fairyland but to nightmares. Her only sugar plum was her thumb which since babyhood had always occupied her bedtime hours and much of her days as well, in spite of the cayenne pepper, thumb stalls, and other sundry devices used to dissuade her from this annoying habit.

So this night started out like any other with the thumb-sucking ritual, and soon she was fast asleep. But something awakened her suddenly--could it have been a knocking? Quietly, in her long white nightie, she slid over the side of her bed and tiptoed--or was it more like floated--past her grandparent's bed, only a few feet away, into the front parlor.

The moonlight filtering through the heavy lace saturated the air like dirty water with shiny bubbles frothing up all around her. Venturing into this room that held such terror for her by day, she was amazingly unafraid, enveloped as she was in this strange protective glow of light. The worn black leather davenport frowned at her through the dim vapor, and the same four eyes from their squares on top of the oak table, leered at her menacingly, as they always did. But then, in the eerie blur, they seemed to drift upward, one to each corner of the ceiling where they hung suspended as if by some magic glue. There they remained, transfixed, inanimate--now harmless to this child of the silver mist.

When she neared the edge of the ornate rug, about two feet from the door, she paused, not sure of her next move. The creak of the polished wood floor might arouse the stern figure slumbering in the adjoining room. But as she reached for the doorknob, it opened as if by an unseen hand, and she eased herself, seemingly without any effort on her part, out onto the screened-in porch. She stared into the evening darkness, searching, hoping, believing--strangely drawn by some powerful force she could not comprehend. It was such a blessed feeling, and she was excited by its promise.

The usually cool mountain air seemed warm as it caressed her small arms. She could see the snow-white hair of Mt. Powell spilling raggedly down its face in the distance. Each starry pinpoint of light winked down through the purple velvet canopy above her head, as if smiling as they gently lit her steps from the porch toward the white strips just visible at the edge of the soft, moist, green carpet before her. She did not know what she would find out there beyond the gate where she was never allowed to go, especially since her grandmother had received that small white piece of paper in the mail. She had heard her grandparents whispering about it, but she remembered only one word of their conversation: "kidnap." The one word seemed to have steeled her grandmother with vigilance although Betty Jane had no idea what it had meant.

As she neared the forbidden gate, she could see a dim dark outline taking shape just beyond. It seemed unable or unwilling to come nearer, but silhouetted in this mystical, ethereal light, its edges glistening with small pearly drops; it appeared to emanate some unearthly strength--some protective force--with the same invincibility of the mountain behind it, and she felt no fear. She had always loved that mountain, and then she thought of her books with pictures of mountains and fairy godmothers. "I wonder if I have a fairy godmother," she thought. Then she wondered if the shape out there could be one, but no, it would not surely come in disguise, would it? But the thought persisted because she sensed that it wanted to give her something.

Now she could see what appeared to be arms reaching for her from its dark brown inner depth, but they were too short to reach beyond the fence. Drawn by this warm comforting force, she just touched the latched gate, and it opened. Then the figure seemed to back away suddenly, shrinking down to her own size, its arms still outstretched; and she thought it would disappear entirely before she could reach it. But it continued to diminish before her eyes, and presently it lay shrunken and lifeless on the sidewalk before her where it had been set just outside the gate earlier that day, its hands immobile, entreating, and still projecting upward. When she approached it, she saw that it had no face; only dents and creases in the area where a face had been once and two spots that had probably been its eyes. Bending over it, she felt suddenly protective towards this creature that seemed to call to her out of her past as if seeking to share some secret happiness that she had known so long ago.

Together, they seemed to float back into the house, and she tumbled sleepily into her little iron bed, lying as quiet and still as if she had never left it.

The next morning, after her grandmother had run the bath water for Betty Jane, she pulled back the covers and said, "Time to get up, child," and looking down exclaimed, "Where on earth did you get that dirty old teddy bear?"

Betty Jane pulled the teddy bear close in her arms and smiled to herself a secret smile.

(Betty J. Lyons)

In considering any potential narrative, we distill the various high points of emotional intensity, isolating a pattern that gradually assumes the basic structure of a plot. We outline the story with succeeding episodes leading to the climax or inevitable conclusion, perhaps the loss of the very thing that the protagonist so dearly sought. But what is the device that moves the story through the various episodes of ascending intensity, maintaining reader interest and building to the final and concluding scene? Simply put, it is conflict between opposing forces that develops tension in the plot, awakens and holds reader interest, and moves the story toward the final resolution in the climax. Without conflict, no plot is really possible, and no story would have wide appeal.

For the purpose of illustration, let us return to the story about William Grant's loss of the postal contract. This incident can be seen as one of two possible conflicts: Grant against himself as his need for public approval wins out over his ethical sense of what is right (man against himself); or Grant in conflict with a public that censures and, in his mind, finally ostracizes him (man against man). The man against nature conflict does not immediately suggest itself here. The writer could really use either conflict, but it is best that whatever he does, he focus on one. The following is the entry from Grant's journal:

> I must here mention a very unpleasant affair that occurred in the Post Office. One of my musical friends, Brother George Rowley, a blind man, for whom I had done many acts of kindness and helped to live all I could had some circulares on organs sent to him and a lot of prices. I had generally acted as his secretary to all such business for him and being mad at the dealer who sent him these circulares, I threw them away, thinking they were only catchpennies and he knew nothing of them. But he did, and I was traced up and as he had threatened I was removed from the Post Office, so I published the circular that is here copied as many false rumors got abroad that damaged my character.

> Removal of the Post Office
> To the Inhabitants of American Fork and Vicinity

> Fellow Citizens:
> You are doubtless aware of the reports in circulation regarding my actions as assistant P.M. of this city. Allow me to say a few words to vindicate myself.
> The reports are with scarcely an exception, untruthful, and the result of ill will on the part of envious persons and surmise by others. In the past I have spared neither efforts, expense nor courtesy to oblige the public while in office. I have never wilfully detained mail matter or interfered with it beyond what may be called reasonable detention or necessary interference.
> I have at great expense created the largest and finest public building in your city and have purchased and erected lock boxes and all other conveniences that would assist the public in a

speedy and safe delivery of the mails.

During the past five years I have had charge of 2,000 registered and probably 100,000 other letters, and have the satisfaction of saying that not one of the registered letters has failed to reach its destination, and I further solemnly assert--on my honor as a God-fearing man--that I have never abstracted from the mails, or defrauded the public of a single cent, but have made it my policy to suffer myself, rather than infringe upon the rights of others, and I defy proof of the contrary.

To those who imagine they have just cause for complaint, I would desire them to call upon me, and I will give satisfactory explanation sufficient to remove all doubts.

That letters may have been lost I do not deny, but thru no fault of mine.

I have been charged with opening a letter, I answer, this by saying I took it for one of mine, as it was similar to what I had received from time to time. I put the circular (on Pianos and Organs) in our waste paper box, and am anxious to make every reparation in my power by replacing said circular.

Another charge is that I have publicly read postal cards. My answer is, whenever I have done so, it was to assist and benefit the public.

This explanation I trust will be acceptable and I hope still to merit the confidence and approbation of an appreciating public.

In closing I will say I have acted as agent for many and have been entrusted with thousands of dollars for papers, merchandise, etc. and no instance has yet arisen where any one has not received all they paid for. Thanking you for past favors, and desiring the welfare and prosperity of the whole people, I remain your obedient servant--William Grant

(American Fork, Oct. 16, 1877)

Scores of people had some little complaint to make, but most of them of a very little and frivolous nature, but nevertheless I valued my good reputation above all price. I deemed it my duty to defend my actions and except in the case mentioned not the slightest charge could be sustained against me, and had I not known that those circulares were worthless to the party addressed and deemed by me swindlers to the community, I should not have thoughtlessly thrown them away. I offered my circulares and prices as he said he wanted to go into business. I offered compensations, but no go. It seemed as he said, he would push me to the utmost. So the Bishop, our post master, took the office away from me. I have often thought and do still think that this case was a trap set by a few jealous enemies to find a cause to injure me and they succeeded well, and I lost thereby an office worth from 6 to 8 hundred dollars a year to me. It made me feel very sick. Nervousness and restlessness set in, and my health was endangered. I felt very feeble for some 6 months after, which was caused by the black looks and bad feelings manifested by some professed friends. Many thot some bad things would come out of this removal, but I did not, as I had done my best for all and acted honorable and more than liberal with the people. There was consequently no case. Many thot it would break me up, and it did hurt me much for I have certainly missed the $600 a year we took in at the office and the business arising therefrom, but I will here say we got bravely over it all, and I do not know but what it was alright in the long run. It left me very weak, however, in the body, and I drank more tea occasionally as a stimulant only.

Now taking into consideration all the information that we have gleaned from the journal, we arrive at a working plot in the following steps:

1. We establish the theme including the basic conflict of the narrative.
2. We list the scenes, building gradually to the climactic scene.
3. We arrange the scenes so as to play down distracting elements and move the story as rapidly as possible to the conclusion of the conflict.
4. We list the details of the scenes.

We have already expressed the theme: William Grant's drive for prestige (ambition) brought him into direct confrontation, first with an old friend and later, by extension, with the society in which he lived. Recognizing that this narrative sets man against man, we outline four possible scenes from the journal:

1. William discovers and angrily discards the circulars.
2. George Rowley confronts William about the missing circulars.
3. Many townspeople accuse William of reading and losing their mail.
4. The bishop relieves William of the postal contract.

There are, obviously, many ways to present the story. We could present all four scenes chronologically, moving from scene 1 through the resolution of the conflict in scene 4. This would assume a longer narrative. For a shorter narrative we could present only the one scene in which the bishop relieves William of the postal contract referring only indirectly to the other three scenes. I have highlighted the vocabulary and syntactical items that I lifted from the journal account and other contemporary sources:

It had been several days since William had seen the bishop, a large, energetic farmer who, in addition to his duties as the town's lay minister, served as the postmaster. William had noticed his *black looks* now for several weeks particularly after the music teacher with *new methods* had moved into town. Too many people were *jealous of William's reputation* as choir leader, not to mention his new music store, and they would do almost anything *to break him up.* Each Sunday, when he came to church, he halfway expected to find *the new man with new ideas* directing the choir. As the bishop thrust himself into the mid-morning clutter of the store, William felt it was not going to be a friendly visit.

He was half-way across the store's *20-by-40 foot* show room before the door banged shut. He stood now, looking down at the much smaller William Grant.

"William," ordered the bishop.

William knew that the bishop could not have helped but notice the store's *large and varied stock;* even *the gallery, which ran completely around the room* and overflowed with merchandise, called out for attention. The music store had done remarkably well with the added assortment of *books, school materials, jewelry, stationery, toys, and glassware.* But it was the postal contract that had pleased him the most; it brought in an extra $600 to $800 a year and allowed him to add *assistant P.M.* to his name. Anyone entering his store on postal business could not help but buy. At times, *William's brain almost whirled with joy with everybody patronizing him.*

"William, there are plenty of people in town who want to know what's been happening to their mail," the bishop stated.

William felt his face flush and the old *nervousness returning.*

"Is this how people in town repay me after I create *the largest and finest public building* in town. What about *all those lock boxes that I erected to assist the public in the delivery of the mail?*"

The bishop refused to be sidetracked. "We all know what you've done, William; but what about George Rowley's circulars from Salt Lake? He claims you throwed them out."

William knew exactly what had happened to those circulars. For years he had *acted as George's* personal *secretary,* helping him with *countless acts of Christian kindness.* He had even *helped him to live.* When George grew ever blinder, he had asked William to take over more and more of his personal business; and then when George had suddenly decided that he was going to start his own music business and had sent away for some circulars on organs and pianos from some *swindlers* back East, William had taken matters in his own hands.

"Bishop," William answered. "I only threw those circulars away because they were absolutely worthless; those people would have *swindled* the entire community." Somehow George had known that William had received the circulars and *traced him up*. And now he had done just as he threatened and told the bishop-postmaster.

"There are plenty of people in this town who are wondering why so much of their mail seems to go lost," the bishop continued.

"Bishop, those were only *catch pennys*. And I offered George *compensations* for the lost circulars, but *no go*."

So his old friend George had sided with his critics in town. There wasn't an ounce of truth to the false *rumors that got abroad*, and now a *few jealous enemies* were all *laying a trap* for him. This was how *professed friends* worked to damage *his character*.

"William, I can't have complaints about you reading postcards and opening mail that don't belong to you. We had better have someone else help with the mail at least until we can figure out what's going on. You know how people talk."

William was now shaking, and as soon as the bishop was gone, he walked to the back of the store where he kept a kettle ready on a stove. *"The loss of the postal business would hurt*, but we will *get bravely over it. Probably in the long run it would be for the better,"* William thought as he began to brew himself some tea. It was not the loss of business that hurt; it was the hypocrisy of the people, his professed friends, and the loss of *his good reputation. "I live among a strange people,"* he heard himself saying as he began to sip the hot, comforting liquid.

Or we might consider the four projected scenes for the best point at which to start a much more extended story, selecting scene 4, the confrontation between William and the bishop-postmaster as the starting scene. Since we have only one basic conflict to resolve—the point at which William loses the contract—we could employ flashbacks to present scenes 1 through 3, moving ultimately to William's being relieved of the postal contract. We could conclude by expressing William's sense of betrayal and paranoia. If we feel very imaginative, we can construct dialogue and details that are only hinted at in the journal; in narrative above, I have largely used, for dialogue, thoughts and statements William left behind in his journal. Actually there is no need to alter the facts or to fabricate details that flesh out some of the incidents hinted at. If we feel strongly about adhering strictly to the historical facts, we might consider researching additional contemporary historical records for more details. The technique is really the same: we make lists of facts, trivia, vocabulary items, syntax, and countless details that we arrangethat we emphasizes the theme or main point, building the narrative to the final resolution of the conflict between William and George Rowley. The process is almost mechanical; if we begin with a basic theme, a brief sketch of the scenes, and adequate, detailed lists, we can normally proceed with a sense of purpose that should result in a workable story.

Chapter 4

Point of View

In writing family history, there are three basic aspects to point of view: the historical perspective or perception through which the story is seen; the historical time and specific place of the story; and the person, first or third, through which the story is presented. Each family history--exposition or narrative--is a marriage of all three elements.

PERSPECTIVE

We all know something about the difference between our modern American culture and more traditional cultures, whether American or foreign. In a traditional culture, loyalties are first to the family, conjugal and extended, while in the modern American culture, particularly the culture of young Americans, loyalties are less to one's family than to one's social peer group. Few modern Americans would consider it their life-long duty to avenge the death of a relative, but a familial blood vendetta in the Middle East, for example, is still today very serious business and can remain alive through several generations. We may not like or understand these "foreign" ways of behaving, thinking, and feeling, but we are mentally prepared to accept the "differentness."

Many of us are far less able or willing, however, to accept the fact that someone living in another part of our country at a slightly different point in time may have had a radically different behaving, thinking, and feeling value system or "culture" than we have today. This is particularly true when we are dealing with someone like grandparents. After all, they were members of our families, touched our lives at least for a few years, and probably were native Americans. But being in the same family and living in the same country does not mean that those persons behaved, thought, or felt the same way we do. Consider the mental gulf that separates a secularized American who lives for the "here and now" and a religiously-oriented American who is convinced that the "end of the world" is nigh. While this preoccupation with an apocalyptic climax to world history is less evident among religious groups today than it was in the nineteenth century, it has enjoyed a recent popularity among some groups in the United States (see William Martin's "Waiting for the End," *The Atlantic*, June, 1982), and we only have to read the newspaper to recognize that it is ultimately the driving force among many Islamic movements in the Middle East. The point is not that one approach is better or more important than the other, but that people of similar religious and national backgrounds (separated by a century or less) may have very different views of life. It does not take a great leap of the imagination to realize that not only did people who lived in the past probably all think differently from us, they also behaved and felt differently.

Much of what we discussed in Chapter 2 on values was an attempt to develop a system for bridging the value gulf between us and a historical subject; however, the other discussions in this chapter are just as important a part of individual and historical perspective. The attempt to establish the peculiar historical perspective of an ancestor is not an easy one because our picture of the inner or personal world of an individual is largely the result of the writer's interpretation of historical documents. Obviously, the journal is the best source of information on how someone viewed the world, but even here the narrator has to be extremely careful if he is to isolate correctly the historical perspective of an ancestor.

One of the most fascinating journals ever kept is that of Samuel Pepys. The entry that he made on Sunday, 25 October 1668 is typical. His wife had surprised Mr. Pepys, locked in an embrace with Deb, a servant girl, in his words with his "hand sub coats." Mrs. Pepys said nothing but rushed from the room. Because Pepys was not absolutely certain that his wife had actually seen him in this compromising entanglement, he elected to ignore the entire incident. About 2 o'clock in the morning, Mrs. Pepys woke him, crying, to tell him that she was secretly a Roman Catholic. Once again Samuel Pepys decided that it was far better for him to ignore this provocative statement, being very much aware that the probable cause of her religious confession was her anger over his indiscretion with the servant girl. By the next night, his wife told him that she had indeed seen him hugging and kissing the girl and demanded that the girl be expelled from the house. Interestingly, Pepys remained firmly unrepentant, for on 13 November he noted in his journal that he was resolved to have Deb's maidenhead. A modern, secular American might understand Pepys, but it is hard to imagine a man more separated from the strict Puritan ethic that characterized so many of his countrymen. For several weeks, the agony between Pepys and his wife continued until on 19 November 1668, Samuel confessed everything to buy marital peace. He even fell to praying albeit not "heartily." But torn still between his desires for the servant girl and his desire to abate his wife's anger, he found himself becoming increasingly depressed. Even the "hanging" of his best chamber did little to revive his spirits. Finally, his passion for the girl did abate, and apparently matters returned to normality. What is intriguing about Pepys is that whatever he did--religious or otherwise--it was simply a guise on his part to gain a little time and some needed marital peace.

What makes Pepys's entries interesting is his very pragmatic and secular moral value system at a time when religion was still an important part of most people's lives. But there are many other interesting questions and answers that give us insight into people of his class and era and help us understand how people thought, felt, and behaved. What was the social value of servants, and was Pepys's conduct with the servant girl typical or atypical of other masters? What exactly did his wife mean about her being secretly a Roman Catholic? What happened to expelled servants, particularly to pregnant ones, and how did the society view and provide for them? We know full well that Pepys's wife did not approve of his approaches to his servant girl, but how would Pepys's masculine contemporaries have viewed his sexual adventurism? Basically, what was Pepys's personal culture or frame of reference, his perspective or view of the world?

Knowing what a person's view of the world was at a particular point in time does not give us a complete picture of the changes that a historical character might have gone through. A mature father about to be hanged for rape would have a very different view of the world than when he was a young revolutionary soldier returning flushed from victories over the British. Journals are excellent sources of a person's inner world, but there are real limitations. William Grant began his journal at the age of forty-four, and his summary at the beginning of the journal of his first forty-four years reflects all the personal optimism and sense of confidence of a man at the peak of his personal powers. He remembers how as a youth he had told his sick-with-cholera and grief-stricken mother that if "she would have faith like me she could be well." This confidence of youth stands in stark contrast with his late-in-life bouts with depression as he grows increasingly isolated from his friends and community. His perspective altered at several points during his life, and his summary of his first forty-four years, while reflecting accurately how he felt at forty-four, obliterates any changes that he underwent during that forty-four-year period. The narrator must carefully work out the personal perspective of a historical character at a particular point in time, and he must be sensitive to the changes in personality and alterations in perspective that took place throughout a person's life.

Not only do people change, but, as we have observed in the case of Samuel Pepys, not everyone living at the same time and in the same area felt or thought the same way. It is widely known that when Charles II was restored to the English throne in 1660, many theatres that had been closed since Cromwell's rise to power in 1642 suddenly reopened to cater to individuals such as Pepys, but it is hard to believe that lovers of the theatre had simply ceased to exist during the time of Oliver Cromwell and his Puritan repression. Samuel Pepys probably had never accepted Puritan values, and people like him must have kept a very low profile during Cromwell's era. While Puritans were amusing themselves reading Bunyan's *Pilgrim's Progress*, Pepys was probably amusing himself chasing pretty servant girls about his estate. The narrator has to be selective in considering information, but it is obvious that even if we can determine generally what a group or a class may have thought or felt, it is not always true that a person living at that time would have viewed the world in a similar fashion. People of similar social groups probably had similar views, but even here there must have been subtle differences. Acknowledging all these limitations, I will suggest some ways to determine the perspective of a historical subject.

One way to become acquainted with how most people thought and felt during a certain time is to examine what people read. In other words, we should know what was popular at the time a person lived. Eleanor Porter's novels about Pollyanna may never be considered great literature, but they found a ready audience because they appealed to the general and popular taste and can therefore be considered a barometer of that age. It has been estimated that millions of copies of McGuffey readers made their way into the minds and hearts of Americans during the second half of the nineteenth century. Because the editors and publishers of these moralistic readers revised the stories to reflect changing values, a writer can (through these readers) plot how most people thought and felt at any particular point in the latter half of the nineteenth century. The editors of these readers chose from great literature--the works of Wordsworth, Milton, and Shakespeare--as well as from traditional Christian and patriotic lore to make moralistic points that reflected the values and popular culture of that age: children should be good and not rude; practice charity and individualism; be kind to animals; play only after finishing lessons and work; take care of one's parents; and recognize God's ruling hand.

Another way to gain some insight into an ancestor's mind is to consider what the ancestor's contemporaries wrote and said in local newspapers. While I may have no personal knowledge as to how my ancestor in Quebec two centuries ago thought, I do have access to poems, songs, and personal letters that appeared in the *Quebec Gazette*, a paper that my ancestor probably read. This paper, typical of thousands upon thousands of other local gazettes, also includes letters written to the paper, giving the researcher insight into what people at that time valued, discussed, and concerned themselves with. It is really not difficult, by reading such a paper, to come up with what a historical character probably did, felt, and thought. Newspaper advertisements are also an excellent source of information. In 1869, the Hooper Brothers took over a store in Chariton, Iowa, from a certain O. L. Palmer. Their advertisements in a local newspaper give us some insight into what people valued and how they viewed the world. Among other things, their advertisements list dress goods; hats or caps; carpets in the latest patterns; tea, sugar, coffee, molasses, tobacco, and rice; and queensware. Here we have not only a view of what a typical store probably sold but also a picture of what people saved their money to buy. The advertisement continues, "20,000 Lives Lost Every Year! By Wearing 'Shoddy' Clothes! 20,000 Dollars Lost Yearly in this Country By buying Poor Boots and Shoes, . . ." It is fascinating to consider the mental world of an individual who could have taken such a "pitch" seriously.

Still another way to understand how a person thought is to determine what was going on in the larger world surrounding a historical character. For example, Joseph Antoine Waller, a male Alsatian teenager in a small village during the early 1830s, would have had related in a very predictable way to the world about him. After determining his ethnic and cultural profile, his economic profile, and his occupational profile, we would still find areas that we could explore that would help us understand his broader, political and social world. His father had recently died, leaving a family at the mercy of constantly recurring famines and international political conflict. To add to the uncertainty, his family was now considering leaving his native village and travelling thousands of miles to a new and unpredictable country. This young man, the son of farmers and laborers, had been raised as a farmer and as a faithful member of the Roman Catholic Church. There were also issues of an even broader nature that were probably impinging on the life of this young Alsatian male. Decisions were being made in Paris and Berlin that would have an impact on his little world. There was the threat of approaching military duty, and there were social revolutions and national upheavals that would soon redefine his world forever. By becoming an astute student of local, regional, and national issues, the family historian develops an extensive list of concerns and issues that would probably have been part of this young man's world. We may never know exactly what the subject of our exposition or narrative thought, felt, and did, but we can with a little patience arrive at a reasonable idea.

Perspective refers to the particular perception--the mindset--that the character or characters in our exposition or narrative had, the vantage point from which that character viewed the world. A historical personality represents a totality--a personal and familial totality as well as a cultural, historical, and physical background--that sets him off from others; in one sense we can think of this totality as a personal culture, an individual's private "value system." Historical influences, cultural orientation, family biases, and personal experience combine to define how a historical personality perceived the world about him.

We have all experienced attempts at exposition or narration that have failed because the author dressed historical figures with modern values and issues. Sigrid Undsett's *Kristin Lavransdatter* is a good example of an author reaching back in time to develop a successful medieval perspective. How did someone think, feel, and behave in four-teenth-century Norway? Consider the following lament from a confused and concerned husband:

She might well make shift with those she hears at home,

methinks," said Erlend. "But 'tis pity of her--as things are going, all youth is being worn away from her." He struck one hand against the other. "I see not how the Lord can think we have need of a new son every year."

(Sigrid Undsett, *Kristin Lavransdatter*)

The author--perhaps I should say the translator--has developed a dialogue style that strikes the reader as quaintly medieval, but the success of the passage results as well from the author's description of the medieval mind's almost superstitious preoccupation with religion and basic simplicity as to matters of human biology. This perspective on life combines with a dialogue style to create a medieval ambience.

There is much more to historical perspective or mindset than being acquainted with general descriptions of the time and area (see the bibliographies in Chapter 2), but broad historical and social-historical works that provide all-important background material are a vital part of the process of arriving at a certain person's perspective in time and place. To facilitate one's control of the various items, I have grouped the following bibliography according to geographic area, but there are still innumerable books and articles that deal with the different regions and eras. The bibliography is highly selective, but it does give some idea of the range and variety of material available.

BIBLIOGRAPHY OF BACKGROUND MATERIALS

JOURNALS AND GENERAL BIBLIOGRAPHIES

American Quarterly

Armstrong, John Borden. *Maine: A Bibliography of Its History*. Boston: G.K. Hall and Company, 1977.

Bassett, T.D. Seymour, ed. *Vermont: A Bibliography of Its History*. Boston: G.K. Hall and Company, 1981.

Crouch, Milton and Hans Raum. *Directory of State and Local History Periodicals*. Chicago: American Library Association, 1977.

Journal of Family History

Journal of Interdisciplinary History

Journal of Marriage and the Family

Journal of Social History

Journal of Urban History

Haskell, Jr., John D. *Massachusetts: A Bibliography of Its History.* Boston: G.K. Hall and Company, 1976.

Haskell, Jr., John D. and T.D. Seymour Bassett. *New Hampshire: A Bibliography of Its History.* Boston: G.K. Hall and Company, 1979.

Historical Methods Newsletter

Kaminkow, Marion J. *United States Local Histories in the Library of Congress.* Baltimore: Magna Carta Book Company, 1975.

Kyvig, David E., and Myron A. Marty. *Nearby History: Exploring the Past Around You.* Nashville: American Association of State and Local History, 1984.

Parks, Roger, ed. *Rhode Island: A Bibliography of Its History.* Hanover and London: University Press of New England, 1983.

Rocq, Margaret M., ed. *California and Local History: A Bibliography and Union List of Library Holdings.* Palo Alto, Calif.: Stanford University Press, 1970.

Signs

William and Mary Quarterly

THE UNITED STATES AND CANADA

Caldwell, Erskine, ed. *American Folkways Series.* New York: Duell, Sloan, & Pearce.
This series in a folksy and light style presents very readable backgrounds on almost every geographic region in the United States. While each author differs in his method of presentation and some are of greater value than others, all generally combine narrative and anecdote with historical description. The emphasis is on capturing the characteristics and culture of the very ordinary people who settled each region.

> *Big Country.* (Donald Day) 1947.
> *Blue Ridge Country.* (Jean Thomas) 1942.
> *Buckeye Country.* (Louise Bromfield).
> *Corn Country.* (Homer Croy) 1947.

Deep Delta Country. (Harnett T. Kane) 1944.
Desert Country. (Edwin Corle) 1941.
Far North Country. (Thames Williamson) 1944.
Gold Rush Country. (Charis Wilson).
Golden Gate Country. (Gertrude Atherton) 1945.
Gulf Coast Country. (Hodding Carter) 1951.
High Border Country. (Eric Thane) 1955.
High Sierra Country. (Lewis Oscar) 1955.
Lower Piedmont Country. (H.C. Nixon) 1946.
Mackinac Country. (Iola Fuller).
Mormon Country. (Wallace Stegner) 1942.
Niagara Country. (Lloyd Graham) 1949.
North Star Country. (Meridel Le Sueur) 1945.
Ozark Country. (Otto Ernest Rayburn) 1941.
Pacific Country. (Richard Neuberger) 1940.
Palametto Country. (Stetson Kennedy) 1942.
Pennsylvania Dutch Country. (Harry Emerson Wiles).
Pinon Country. (Alfred Powers) 1949.
Rocky Mountain Country. (Albert Nathaniel Williams) 1950.
Short Grass Country. (Stanley Vestal) 1941.
Southern California Country. (Carey McWilliams) 1946.
Wheat Country. (William B. Bracke) 1950.

Cary, John H. and Julius Weinberg. *The Social Fabric.* Vol. I: *American Life from 1607 to the Civil War* and Vol. II: *American Life from the Civil War to the Present.* Boston: Little, Brown and Company, 1978.
A series of essays on American social history, "touching upon marrying and making love, fighting and getting drunk, owing the grocer, and going without heat."

Diffenderffer, Frank Ried. *The German Immigration into Pennsylvania Through the Port of Philadelphia from 1700 to 1775.* Baltimore: Genealogical Publishing Co., 1977.
A general history with a local and family history orientation.

Holli, Melvin G. and Peter d'A Jones. *The Ethnic Frontier: Essays in the History of Group Survival in Chicago and the Midwest.* Grand Rapids, Mich.: William B. Eerdmans Publishing Co., 1977.
A series of background essays on the various ethnic groups that made up the city of Chicago and the Midwest in general.

Jones, Rufus H. *The Quakers in the American Colonies.* New York: Russell & Russell, 1962.
A historical study of the Quaker movement, focusing on New England and the southern colonies in general and New York, New Jersey, and Pennsylvania in particular.

The Making of America. National Geographic Society.
A series of seventeen maps showing the economic, political, and social history of the regions of the United States: New England, Central Plains, Southwest, Far West, Hawaii, Ohio Valley, Texas, Northern Plains, Atlantic Gateways, and Alaska

The Sears, Roebuck Catalogue.
Richard Sears issued his first mail-order catalogue in 1891, and various publishers have in recent years reproduced various issues. Crown Publishers published most of the 1902 edition, and Digest Books, published the Fall 1900 issue. Other publishers have issued selected pages from certain years. These catalogues are wonderful picture windows into everyday life. The family narrator will find them useful for almost any kind of narration dealing with America at the turn of the century.

van der Zee, Henri and Barbara. *A Sweet and Alien Land: the Story of Dutch New York.* New York: The Viking Press, 1978.
This book recounts the Dutch colony from the purchase of Manhattan to the surrender to the English in 1664. While much of the book deals with larger figures, the authors do explore the character of the common settler who developed the colony.

Woodward, William E. *The Way our People Lived.* New York: E. P. Dutton & Company, 1944.
In a combination of narration and historical description, the author shows how the common man lived, worked, and played--his manners and customs--over a time span of three centuries.

THE BRITISH ISLES

Cockburn, J.S. *Western Circuit Assize Orders: 1629-1648.* London: Royal Historical Society, 1976.
A collection of orders issued by the Western Circuit Court, which was held periodically in counties of England to try civil and criminal cases.

Elton, Geoffrey Rudolph. *The Sources of History: England, 1200-1640.* Ithaca: Cornell University Press, 1969.
A study of English historical records, focusing on narratives and state, church, legal, and private documents. A necessary background for the family historian and narrator who wants to work with English records.

Great Britain Historical Manuscripts Commission. *Report on the Pepys Manuscripts Preserved at Magdalene College, Cambridge.* London: H.M.S.O., 1911.
A collection of state papers.

Great Britain Public Record Office. *Calendar of State Papers: Domestic Series* (starting 1574) and *Colonial Series* (starting 1574).
The Domestic Series derives from the office of the Secretary of State for the Home Department, while the Colonial Series derives from the Colonial Office. These papers--a collection of correspondence and minutes--are a treasure mine of information about English domestic affairs and the history of New England.

Hey, David G. *An English Rural Community: Myddle under the Tudors and the Stuarts.* Leicester: Leicester University Press, 1974.
A social and economic history of the community of Myddle in Shropshire with an emphasis on the farmers and craftsmen of the village as well as an examination of the intellectual world of the village with a reconstruction of its families and kinship groups.

Hilton, R.H. *A Medieval Society: The West Midlands at the End of the Thirteenth Century.* New York: John Wiley & Sons, 1966.
This book focuses on the social classes and urban development of the diocese of Worcester (counties of Warwick, Worcester, and Gloucester).

MacFarlane, Alan, ed. *The Diary of Ralph Josselin: 1616-1683.* London: The Oxford University Press, 1976.
Ralph Josselin, vicar of Earls Colne, Essex, with his references to people and places in his parish, records an intimate record of his ministry, thus providing a complex picture of himself and of his environment.

Parker, Rowland. *The Common Stream.* London: William Collins Sons & Co., Ltd., 1975.
A history of Foxton, a small village near Cambridge, from the villas of the Romans through the Middle Ages and up through World War II.

Short, Thomas. *New Observations on City, Town and Country Bills of Mortality: London, 1750.* Germany: Gregg International Publishers Limited, 1973.
An analysis by an eighteenth-century physician of the baptism, marriage, and burial register of over 160 county parishes and fifty market towns, this book covers almost any subject one would care to know about seventeenth- and eighteenth-century England. There are even sections on the Bible and meteorology.

Tawney, Richard Henry and Eileen Power. *Tudor Economic Documents; Being Select Documents Illustrating the Economic and Social History of Tudor England.* 3 Vols. London: Longmans, Green and Co., 1924.

A collection of economic documents--agriculture, towns and crafts, corn trade, textiles, mining, manufactures, and foreign trade--relating to the Tudor period, 1485 to 1603.

The Victoria History of the Counties of England. Reprinted for the University of London Institute of Historical Research by Dawsons of Pall Mall Cannon House, Folkestone, Kent, England, 1970.

A national survey of the counties of England from the earliest times, these local and family histories include a wealth of illustrations and cover topography; archaeology; natural history, flora and fauna; Roman and ancient earthworks; the *Domesday Survey;* political, ecclesiastical, social, and economic history; architecture; folklore; manorial history; accounts of the land and its owners from the Conquest to the present day; biography; historic and local families; social life; and manufacturing and industrial developments.

TIME AND PLACE

A natural extension of a discussion on historical perspective is time and place. Except for establishing the personal perspective of the subject of the exposition or narrative, time and place are perhaps the most important elements in any discussion of point of view. And it is obvious that historical perspective is closely linked with time and place. C. Hugh Holman, in his *A Handbook to Literature,* lists the elements that make up the exposition's or narrative's time and place as "the actual geographic location, its topography, scenery, and such physical arrangements as the location of windows and doors in a room"; "the occupations and daily manner of living of the characters"; "the time or period in which the action takes place, e.g. epoch in history, season of the year, etc."; and "the general environment of the characters, e.g. religious, mental, moral, social, and emotional conditions through which the people in the narrative move." In arriving at an understanding of the perspective of the subject or subjects of the narrative, we have already touched on many of these items. Certainly the sources of personal perspective are the same as for time and place, but it is important that the family narrator recognize that knowing what a character thought, did, and felt is still not exactly the same as knowing the details about the time and place in which the story occurred. In each of the student examples below the basic plot is identical, and although there is little character development, the different time and place details create a totally different effect in each version of the same story:

About noon, a cold arctic wind burst over the prairie community of Benton Township, South Dakota, putting a sudden end to the warm autumn day. Before noon, Robert Foster and one of his sons had saddled their horses to visit Robert's brother at a farm a mile or so distant. Because of the sudden storm, they were unable to return for almost two days; when they did, they found the front door to their home wide open with snow piled high in the living room. Robert frantically searched the house for his wife and children, finally finding his wife and one child buried beneath a pile of thick comforters and patch quilts, alive but half frozen from the thirty-six hour ordeal. His wife told Robert that the other two children, Robert Jr. and Sarah, had set out before the storm to check their coyote traps, dressed only for the warm autumn day. She had gone to the door time after time after the storm had arisen, trying to see the two children through the violent curtain of snow until the snow had piled so high in the doorway that she had been unable to close the door. With snow now invading the house and the temperatures falling rapidly, she had dressed herself and the one remaining child in several layers of clothing and gone to bed with all the bedding in the house piled on top of them.

All through the winter the two missing children failed to return, and both Robert and his wife eventually gave up hope of ever seeing them alive. Several months later Robert, while gunning down a chicken-eating coyote, discovered the grisly fate of the children. After he had tracked the predator for miles in the thawing snow of spring, he came across an old claim shack on a neighboring farm. Forcing open the door, he was able to make out in the shack's corner a small form. As his eyes became accustomed to the darkness, he realized that the form was his son, Robert Jr. standing, half naked, over his younger sister, her stiff body still wrapped in Robert's outer garment.

In this story, the student has, through the use of specific details that delineate the time and the place--arctic wind bursting over the prairie community, comforters and patch quilts, coyote traps, the invading snow, and the old claim shack on a neighboring farm, given the story a sense of realism. Now consider the same story with the details altered so as to set the story in a different place and a different time:

About noon, the first shock waves hit the dense southern California communities of the San Fernando Valley. A few minutes before noon, Bob Foster and one of his sons had decided to drive a mile to visit Bob's brother. When the earthquake began to collapse structures, topple telephone and electrical lines, and uproot trees, it made travel on the freeways and surface streets hazardous, and Bob and his son had to spend almost one hour maneuvering the fallen

debris before they were able to return home. They found the front
door to their home partially filled with debris and all the windows
broken out. Alarmed, Bob searched the house for his wife and
children. After a few frantic moments he discovered his wife and
one child still huddled in the doorway to one of the back bedrooms.
His wife told Bob that the other two children, Bob Jr. and Sarah,
had set out just before the earthquake in the family car to do some
shopping at the mall. After the first shock waves, she had wanted to
look for the children but had only made it to the front door when
the earthquake came again. With the returning violent shocks, she
had retreated with the one remaining child to the safety of one of
the bedroom doorways.

Bob immediately set out to see if he could locate the children.
After retracing the route between their home and the mall at least
two times, he caught a glimpse of the family car buried beneath what
looked like a fallen wall. Picking his way through the debris and
forcing open the door to the car, he could see the motionless forms
of his two children. As his eyes became accustomed to the dimness
of the interior, he realized that his son had protectively arched his
body over his sister's face whose still body lay covered in chunks of
glass and stone.

Here the time element is rapidly speeded up from several months to
only a few hours. The coyote traps, horses, primitive conditions, and inability to cope with the storm are replaced with the wonders of communication telescoping days into minutes. The success of a story
depends not only on understanding the perspective of the individual
subjects of the narrative but just as vitally on the author's ability to
recreate accurately the details of the time and the place of the exposition
or narrative. Perhaps there is no point at which beginning students fail
more surely than in thinking that an abstract generalization does the job
of vital and specific details. One professional example will suffice. In
Elisha Partridge's inventory, two wood-working tools are listed: jackknife and gimlets. A "gimlet" was a boring tool; and of course, we all
recognize how one could use a jackknife to work wood. Not much information, but consider how Vilhelm Moberg uses his detailed knowledge
of woodworking tools:

Early every weekday morning Nils emerged from the spare
room, hobbling along on his crutches, slowly reaching his old
workbench outside in the woodshed, where he remained through
the day. He cut spokes for wagon wheels, he made rakes and handles for axes and scythes. He could still use plane and chisel; his
hands were in good health, and their dexterity remained. He taught
Karl Oskar what he could of this handicraft.

(Vilhelm Moberg, *The Emigrants*)

In summary then, vivid and accurate details of geography, occupations, "the actual historical period," and "the general environment of the characters" must all combine to give the exposition or the narrative the ambience of historical time and place.

PERSON

We have defined perspective as the peculiar perception or view of life of a person at a certain time and place, and we have considered the importance of detailing specifically the historical place and time. Point of view, however, also has to do with the way in which the story is presented, namely whether it is being told by the person who experienced it (first person), or whether it is a story about someone else (third person). While there are many variations and subtle shades in either first or third person, most writers of family history use one of the following: first person, in which the narrator relates the story as a witness of the events, evaluating persons and events on the basis of his own very personal powers of perception; third person limited, in which the narrator relates the story in the third person, evaluating and seeing characters and events in the story externally without entering into their minds or limited to external powers of analysis; or third person omniscient, in which the narrator relates the story in the third person, entering the minds of one or several characters and reporting their thoughts and feelings or, in other words, moving freely as to place, character, or time. These distinctions should become clearer if we consider examples of each.

Obviously, first person works best when the narrator is telling his own life story. A first person narrator tells and sees the events of the story exclusively from his limited and very personal point of view. His observations about others reveal a certain naivete, a perspective imposed by his own limited and filtering powers of perception. Russell Baker's *Growing Up* is an autobiography, but Baker does not limit himself to telling his story alone. He tells his mother's story along with his; and when he tells her story, he does not enter her mind but moves and comments from his own point of view or as an external observer:

> At the age of eighty my mother had her last bad fall, and after that her mind wandered free through time. Some days she went to weddings and funerals that had taken place half a century earlier. On others she presided over family dinners cooked on Sunday afternoons for children who were now gray with age. Through all this she lay in bed but moved across time, traveling among the dead decades with a speed and ease beyond the gift of physical science.
> "Where's Russell?" she asked one day when I came to visit at the nursing home.
> "I'm Russell," I said.

She gazed at this improbably overgrown figure out of an inconceivable future and promptly dismissed it.

(Russell Baker, *Growing Up*)

At this point it may be the mother's story, but the narrator is the son who makes external observations in telling the story; and it is through his limited vision or by the means of his limited first person point of view that we see and understand his mother.

There are many advantages to the first person, but for autobiography or biography it is obviously particularly useful. As a person tells his own story, he can range between his perspective as a youth and as a mature adult contrasting these two phases in his life. One could tell William Grant's early experiences of boundless optimism from his late-in-life perspective of hopeless despair. Perhaps most important, the teller of a story can, through first person, involve the reader emotionally in the events of the narrator's story. Consider the following student example of first person point of view:

My father had been working in the copper mill only a short time when my uncle appeared at the bottom of the canyon. I watched him pick his way carefully up the rocky creek bed wondering why he seemed to take so long to reach the top of the grade. By the time he reached the door of our boxcar home, my mother had been standing several minutes waiting in the hot, dusty sun. I saw him carefully place a soiled letter into the protruding hand of my mother who stood just outside the front door. I listened as my uncle explained that my father had accidentally caught his pant leg on a bolt on one of the crushers and been pulled into the machinery and killed. I can remember wondering if that meant that my father would be coming home that weekend.

The emotional reactions are those of the son, and we enter the world of the child, empathizing with the naivete which prevents him from grasping the full significance of the tragic death of his father. Notice that we see the events or other characters, particularly the mother, externally. We do not enter the mind of the mother judging and evaluating everything from the limited point of view of the first person narrator.

In family history, the other commonly used option is third person limited or omniscient. We have defined third person limited as narrating a story without entering the actual minds of characters. Most of the narratives or expositions that amateur family historians write are presented from this point of view. The author moves freely to any place at any time, but he does not enter the minds of his character or characters. While the story "Olin" begins in the first person, the narrator, after four paragraphs, shifts to third person limited. He simply relates the events of the story introducing statements of judgment and evaluation but never once entering into the minds of any of his characters. The family exposition, "My Pioneer Grandmother, Margaret Friday Redman," is also presented from the third person limited point of view. Because many family researchers feel so strongly about writing only what they can legitimately and historically verify, the third person limited is very common and popular with amateur family writers. In fact, we could appropriately define it as the story teller's point of view.

John Egerton's *Generations: An American Family* (Lexington: University Press of Kentucky, 1983) is an interesting example of the mixing of first and third person to present a family history. Chapter 1: "The Last Ones Left" is written entirely in the first person; it is actually an oral history interview that the author conducts. Then in Chapter 2: "Curtis Burnam Ledford," Curtis Ledford proceeds to tell his story, of course in the first person. However, he begins with his great-grandfather, Aley Ledford, and in telling Aley Ledford's story, the author shifts to the third person. Still, the teller of the tale, Curtis Ledford, constantly shifts back to the first person as he breaks what is essentially an expository account with his own personal observations. The shifting between first and third person works because the purpose of the story is as much to have people tell stories about themselves as about others; we, therefore, do not mind the constant editorializing by the story teller:

> He was nineteen years old, and he had a new bride, Elizabeth Farmer--they called her Betsy. She was two years younger than him. Aley's parents were leading the way. I don't know what their names were, but I think his father might have been John Ledford. Anyway, there was three or four families of them in the wagon train--Ledfords, Farmers, Skidmores, Smiths, maybe six or seven wagons in all, including a family of slaves.

However, there is a real danger in this approach. The first person narrator can become what is commonly referred to as the obtrusive narrator constantly and irritatingly introducing himself with editorial and preaching comments into the flow of the narrative. Once again, it works here because of the oral history nature of the book, but it should be used with care.

The third person omniscient narrator can, as with the limited third person, be everywhere and at any time, but there is one important difference. The omniscient narrator enters the minds of his characters. Obviously, the third person omniscient enters the true realm of the fiction writer, and as such it offers wonderful opportunities and challenges. It works best when we have a record of the personal thoughts of an ancestor, the best example being a journal. The short piece about William Grant is an example of the narrator on the basis of a journal record entering the mind of a historical character:

"There are plenty of people in this town who are wondering why so much of their mail seems to go lost," the bishop continued.

"Bishop, those were only catchpennies. And I offered George compensations for the lost circulares, but no go."

So his old friend George had sided with his critics in town. There wasn't an ounce of truth to the false rumors that got abroad, and now a few jealous enemies were all laying a trap for him. This was how professed friends worked to damage his character.

Yet even though we have the journal record, we have no way of knowing whether William Grant ever thought such thoughts in such a context. Many family writers will therefore have nothing to do with the third person omniscient.

Normally, the person choice--first or third--is decided by the circumstances: if the author is telling his own story, autobiography, it would be first person; if he is telling the story of his ancestors, it would be third person. The more important decision seems to be the perspective-- limited to external perceptions or entering the mind of a character in the story and commenting at will in an omniscient mode. One way to practice third person omniscient point of view is to write the same story from a different person's mind or perception. One student wrote an account about an ancestor who lived over 200 years ago in Quebec and about whom he had only the barest of historical information. He knew that his ancestor Henry had married a French-Canadian woman named Jeanne probably in Quebec around 1765 and had had a boy named John around 1766, that this ancestor had possibly served with Wolfe at the Battle of Quebec in 1759, and that he had formed a friendship either during the war or thereafter with a bachelor named William Warren. He also knew that Henry ran a tavern called "The Sign of the Bell" and that William Warren was probably one of his suppliers of rum. Finally, he knew that when Henry and his wife, along with William Warren and several other settlers, left Quebec in the fall of 1767 to settle Ile St. Jeane (later Prince Edward Island), Henry drowned while attempting to come ashore, leaving his pregnant wife alone with their young son to face the uncertainties of the hostile frontier. Shortly thereafter, Jeanne gave birth to her second child and married William Warren. There is no historical evidence to permit us to assume anything other than that this was a marriage of necessity and convenience even though much wilder imaginations might suggest far darker conclusions. Assuming these basic facts, the student wrote the following paragraphs describing the events during the late summer of 1767 when Henry announced in the *Quebec Gazette* the sale of his tavern. These paragraphs are in the third person limited point of view, first from Henry's perspective and then from Jeanne's perspective:

When Henry reached his rooms at the top of the stairs above the tavern "The Sign of the Bell" in Quebec's lower town, he was surprised to find his wife packing all they owned in a large wooden crate. He had only a few days before advertised in the *Quebec Gazette* for a buyer for the tavern, but he never expected to find a buyer so soon. He knew that they would have to leave Quebec for Ile St. Jeane soon if they wanted to be settled in before winter came, but he had expected that it would take days if not weeks to convince his wife to leave Quebec. He had never fit in with the hostile French largely because of his tavern and his tenure as one of the town constables. "I'll tell her later," he had told his friend and rum supplier William Warren as they had reflected with excitement on the cheap land and new opportunities for wealth that lay ahead.

Now from Jeanne's perspective:

Jeanne had seen her husband descending the hill through the open tavern door although she kept her head down while her hands busily poked blankets and linens into the corners and spaces of the crate. She had learned only that morning from the young bachelor Captain William Warren that her husband had found a buyer for the tavern and that he had gone off to make shipping arrangements for the voyage to Ile St. Jeane. She was not pleased that Henry had not discussed the move with her, and she did not like the idea of leaving Quebec and their comfortable three-story stone house with winter coming on. "You could have at least told me first," she said without lifting her head as Henry entered their rooms above the tavern. In truth the only thing that made the whole adventure palatable was that it involved more than just her and her husband. "Making such a drastic move did not seem so frightening if it meant that friends like Captain Warren would join them," she thought as she arranged her personal belongings in a separate space away from her husband's.

The same story could be told from first person point of view either from the perspective of the husband or the perspective of the wife. Actually, the gradation ranging from first to third person can be very subtle. Someone telling his own story could intersperse his own experiences with subjective, disjointed, and very personal observations--much as a journal is written, or he could with less subjectivity tell his own story, avoiding personal observations. In a more objective vein, the author could tell the story from the third person but using the very distinctive perspective of one of the characters, much as the student did in the examples above. A bit more objective would be exposition that works from a thesis or controlling idea. The most objective and least personal form would be the chronicle, which simply lists or presents the facts of the story. Above all, though, avoid the obtrusive narrator. Summaries may work well in exposition, but they can be overpowering particularly when the author cannot avoid preaching or sermonizing. And finally, each writer of family history must recognize that the perspective or the person he chooses is a result of the information he has at his disposal. It is good fun to play with the point of view or perspective of the narrative or exposition, but we must all realize that it is only when and if we have done good historical and family research that we will find ourselves in the happy position of deciding these issues. And then the sources themselves will have probably made the decision for us.

Chapter 5

Some Finishing Touches

Throughout this book, I have emphasized really one thing, namely that the successful family exposition or family narrative results from total immersion in the character and period about which one is writing. In some ways this is so obvious that it seems almost unnecessary to repeat. Yet there are still countless students who begin their family histories without adequate research. Irving Stone made this point in the bibliography in his historical biography *Those Who Love*, the history of Abigail and John Adams. He divided his extensive list of sources into several sections that follow: books containing letters by Abigail Adams; books about Abigail Adams; books by John Adams; books about John Adams; documents and government publications; general histories of the United States and England; specialized histories about the time period (1761 through 1801); Tories; general and specialized studies of the Revolutionary War; the French Revolution; cities; religion; American thought; architecture; clothing; commerce and industry; education; law; life in New England; literature and cultural life; music; New England houses; science and medicine; slavery and servitude; travel; and biographies, autobiographies and writings. He had totally immersed himself in the personalities and period about which he wrote. Total immersion allows the writer to take on literally the character and perspective of his historical subjects. If there is one point that I want to make over and over again, it is simply this: successful characterization and sound historical perspective will only result if the writer does his homework. Even a plot with an arresting conflict resolution is made more possible when the writer knows what really did happen in the historical past. Once again, the writer may begin with genealogical research, but he must augment that research with extensive local and general social, cultural, economic, scientific, and historical research if he expects to produce a successful exposition or narrative. It will happen no other way.

Now that you have finished your story, you still have a few last-minute but important considerations. Most of these come under the general heading of revision, and if you have a personal computer and have used a word-processing program, you will find this normally unpleasant task a much easier one. Ben Johnson wrote that Shakespeare never "blotted a line"; and if this was true, Shakespeare was apparently able in some way to finalize his plays in his mind before he took pen in hand. There is probably no one else in the history of our language about whom that claim can be made, although it is commonly said that Mozart never made a change once he had written music down. For most of us writing is an arduous task filled with countless revisions and rewrites. Recent advances in personal computing, specifically with the numerous excellent word-processing programs available, make the checking of spelling, the movement of sections of text, the reduction and expansion of sentences and ideas, and the final preparation of a camera-ready copy a cinch. Mozart reportedly told his father that a musical composition was finished--he had only to write it down, and in some ways the modern writer can achieve much the same creative control with the computer. He can expand, reduce, rearrange and finalize what he is writing on the computer screen, give a "save" command, and print out a "perfect" final copy. In this sense, the computer seems to aid the natural creation process. The outline is an important first step (we should never forget this), but some writers need to see the actual story or composition before the mind will dictate the final form. The combination of sentences, the flow of ideas, and the very form of the piece of writing gives birth to new ideas, phrases, and sentences. The narrative itself becomes an inspiration and a creative step to further creative leaps; writing is a somewhat circular process. In all this, the computer becomes a natural aid in the creative process. We may never be able to achieve the creative genius of a Shakespeare or a Mozart, but with the modern convenience of word-processing programs, we are in a position to explore, with ease and facility, all our own native creative talents.

Still the writer must have the determination to continue developing his narrative through revision after revision. Anyone who has taught a college course knows the serious limitation that time imposes on the revision process. And anyone who has been forced to make a living knows how little time there is left in the day to write and revise. Just as the professional writer has the time and energy to synthesize thousands of sources, so does he also have the time and the dedication to spend more time revising the final product. No matter how much easier modern technology may make the task, it still ultimately comes down to the writer's refusal to give up until he has written the kind of story that he can be pleased with. As you revise, however, there are some basic points to keep in mind.

Firstly, there is the accuracy of the research. Unlike other pieces of writing, the family exposition and the family narrative are closely linked with careful and extensive genealogical and family research, and the family writer should ask himself if he has done sufficient research so that his exposition or narrative will be a historically accurate piece of writing.

One of my students once wrote a narrative about the antebellum South when the slaves rode carts to the swamps where they harvested reeds with sickles. The details were so inaccurate that no one could take the story seriously. This concerns also how you dress your characters, how you have them speak, and how you have them behave. Also what about the setting, the time and the place? Was the action reasonable and consistent with the people who lived at that time? And does the story make logical sense--not logical sense as we might expect it to be today, but logical sense at that time and at that place? All these are concerns that we have addressed and discussed over and over throughout this book, but the narrator needs to be reminded of them constantly, particularly if he ever hopes to write a convincing family exposition or narrative.

Secondly, (and this applies more specifically to the narrative), the writer should ask himself, when he revises, whether he has organized the narrative so that the story proceeds with the right pace. Have some scenes been slighted while others dragged on too long? Beginning the story in the right place and organizing the sequence of scenes in the right order are both part of the problem, but ultimately this concerns the rate at which the author reveals information. We all feel that many novels of the last century moved too slowly, yet we feel equally cheated by the fast pace of the television story. As you revise, ask yourself if the scenes in your narrative include unnecessary action, redundant parts, or unnecessary characters. And ask yourself if you have sufficiently explored scenes. The point is that you must move the story along at a comfortable pace.

Thirdly, consider your diction. Do you use words of an Anglo-Saxon or Latin origin? Do you used overworked phrases or words? Have you avoided the trite and the cute? Have you considered the length of your sentences? Here it is important to have others read what you write and to listen to your narrative in the mouths of others. Above all, know what other authors have written. Analyze their style; understand their diction.

Lastly, have you said something worth saying? Is your theme fresh and evocative? Have you let your reader think? Many of my students justify poorly written narratives or expositions by arguing that they are written just for the family. The fact is that though our immediate family members may now make up for our sloppiness with understanding, there will come a day when the members of our families will not understand the narratives and expositions we have left behind unless we write them well. Essentially, we are writing so that we will not be forgotten by those who love us and whom we have loved. Write well; it may be your only chance to be remembered.

INDEX

Notes

Notes

Before you begin writing your family narrative,
get the new companion book to
Writing the Family Narrative–

Writing the Family Narrative
WORKBOOK

The *Workbook* shows you how to apply what you
learned in *Writing the Family Narrative* and walks
you step-by-step through the process of writing
your family's story. The book is filled with excellent family writing examples from professional and
novice writers, and provides an array of specific
writing exercises where you can make tangible
progress on your own family story. Available in fall
1993 from Ancestry®.

To order, or for more information,
call 1-800-ANCESTRY® today!